The Midterms
Why They Are So Important
and So Ignored

The Midterms
Why They Are So Important and So Ignored
by
Earl Ofari Hutchinson

PRESS

The Midterms Why They Are So Important and So Ignored

Copyright © 2022 Earl Ofari Hutchinson
All rights reserved including the right of reproduction in whole or in part in any form.

Printed in the United States

Published by
Middle Passage Press
5517 Secrest Drive
Los Angeles, California 90043

Graphic Design by Alan Bell
Index by Middle Passage Press Index Services

Publisher's Cataloging-in-Publication Data

Names: Hutchinson, Earl Ofari.
Title: The midterms : why they are so important and so ignored / Earl Ofari Hutchinson.
Description: Los Angeles, CA : Middle Passage Press, 2022. | Includes bibliographical references and index.
Identifiers: LCCN 2022909412 | ISBN 9781088061978 (pbk.)
Subjects: LCSH: Direct democracy—United States. | Elections—United States. | Voting—United States. | BISAC: POLITICAL SCIENCE / American Government / General. | POLITICAL SCIENCE / Political Process / Campaigns & Elections. | POLITICAL SCIENCE / Civics & Citizenship.
Classification: LCC JK1976.H88 2022 | DDC 324.9 H—dc23
LC record available at https://lccn.loc.gov/2022909412

Library of Congress Control Number: 2022909412
Middle Passage Press, Los Angeles, California

Table of Contents

1	Introduction
7	The Tortured History of the Midterms
28	The President's Party Midterm Nosedive
55	The GOP's Midterm Bullseye
71	Culture Wars, Vote Suppression, and Messaging
86	The Disappearing Voter
114	Breaking the Democrats' Midterm Jinx
137	Warring on Voting Rights
158	Destroying Two Presidents
181	Conclusion Midterm Lessons
198	Postscript The 2014 Versus 2022 Midterms
206	Appendix
212	Notes
248	Bibliography
255	Index
263	About the Author

The Midterms
Why They Are So Important
and So Ignored

Introduction

"If we don't do that it's going to be a sad, sad two years. Think about Republicans if they controlled the Congress these last two years." If the message from President Biden to the members of the Democratic National Committee sounded like it had a note of alarm to it, that's because it did. The occasion was the DNC's winter meeting in Washington, D.C. in March 2022. Biden was deeply concerned that Democrats were not doing enough to assure that they kept control of Congress in the upcoming congressional midterm elections in November 2022.

Biden sounded the alarm bell about the midterms for two very troubling reasons. One, given the long and mostly disastrous history of midterm performance for the president's party, the odds were better than good that the following would happen. The president's party would lose one, or both wings of Congress. At best, his party would suffer some losses.

In every midterm election since World War II, the

scorecard on losses for the president's party has been nothing short of astounding. The average loss for the president's party is twenty-six seats in the House, and four in the Senate. Only six presidents, Woodrow Wilson, Franklin D. Roosevelt, John F. Kennedy, Richard Nixon, Bill Clinton, and George Bush Jr. saw their party hold onto or make gains in the midterms. Fine-tuning that dismal history, even more, only Roosevelt in 1934, and George W. Bush in 2002, registered gains in midterm seats in both houses for their parties.

FDR and Bush's midterm gains, though, are somewhat misleading. In 1934 America was in the near-death grip of the Great Depression and FDR had won a landslide election victory in 1932. His New Deal was widely cheered and did much to take some of the harshest edge off the country's Depression woes. In 1934, he was still riding the crest of popularity. Millions of voters in part trusted him and the Democrats to best deliver on their promise to fulfill the desperate need for jobs and economic recovery.

Bush rode the same crest of popularity in 2002 with his still sky-high approval ratings following the shell shock of the 9/11 terrorist attacks. Bush vowed to wage a take no prisoners war on terrorism. Voters believed him and regarded him as a tough wartime like President.

There was another reason Biden was explicit in warning the DNC that there would be much sadness if the Democrats lost the House and or Senate in 2022. A Republican-controlled Congress could dither, duck, dodge, and obstruct any and every initiative and piece of legislation that he proposed. It could block his administration's appointments to key administrative department heads, and judicial appointments. The most crucial being the SCOTUS.

Senate Minority Leader Mitch McConnell flatly pledged a replay of his thwart of former President Obama's legislative initiatives during his last two years in office from 2014 to 2016 if the GOP won back the Senate in the 2022 midterms. When the subject of the confirmation of a Biden pick to the SCOTUS came up, and if he again held the Senate Majority post, McConnell was blunt, "I think it's highly unlikely." He meant his words. He blocked Merrick Garland, Obama's pick to the High Court, in 2016.

* * * * *

When Biden warned about the absolute importance of the midterms to him and the Democrats, he had to be thinking about the horror that former President Obama faced during his second term from 2012 to 2016. The GOP snatched back both the House and the Senate during the 2014 midterm elections. It held tightly to them during Obama's second term. It blocked dozens of his judicial appointments, most importantly his nomination of Garland to the SCOTUS.

Obama got through almost no new legislative initiatives in his final White House days. The 2014 midterm Democratic defeats ensured that his administration was an administration in little but name only. In other words, it was a lame-duck administration two years before his term officially ended.

Biden had much cause for worry. History abundantly showed that the party in power—in 2022 it was the Democrats—almost always lost seats sometimes lots of seats to the other party. At times, this resulted in a flip of Congress to the other party. Polls in early 2022 showed that GOP voters were much more fired up about the 2022 midterms and the prospect of seizing back Congress than Democratic voters. Polls also found that the public generally agreed that the party that controls Congress controls the government. Polls also found substantial agreement among Democrats that they should control Congress. Conversely, Republicans agreed that they should control Congress.

Opinion was divided over which was better, a unified Congress in which Democrats or Republicans controlled both wings of Congress. Or there was a divided Congress in which the Democrats controlled one wing and the GOP the other. Unfortunately, this was a sure prescription for even more congressional turbulence.

If the Democrats lost just one seat in the Senate in 2022, they lost control of the Senate. If they lost just a relative handful of seats in the House, the same. Control was lost. The midterms then were almost literally a matter of political life and death for the Democrats and Biden.

Yet, given the outsized importance past and present of the midterms in determining the shape and direction of the country, why have millions of voters taken them so lightly, if not outright ignored them? The evidence for this is the repeat pattern of the low to sometimes abysmal voter turnout in the midterms, particularly among Black, Hispanic, and young voters.

There are legions of books that examine the presidential elections, and the issues, the personalities, and the pitched battles the presidential candidates and their parties have fought during those elections. However, in my extensive research on the rich and checkered history, enormous political impact, and colossal struggles political parties have waged over the midterms, I was struck by the near nonexistence of any books examining the midterm's tremendous importance to the political shape of the country.

I provide a revealing, in-depth examination of why the midterm elections for Congress, as well as tens of thousands of state and local offices, are so important to both parties. I assess the issues such as the chronic low turnout of voters, especially Black, Hispanic, and young voters, and the resultant deepening political polarization. He details why the GOP has had phenomenal success in mobilizing and energizing its voters for the midterms.

There's an ominous note to that success going forward, "I think that people are very angry. I think you're underestimating the anger of the people on the right." This is Donald Trump speaking in an interview he gave after his 2020 presidential defeat. It underscores that point. Hutchinson discusses Trump's continuing impact on the GOP and how that casts a foreboding shadow on politics in America.

I tell why the midterms during much of their history have flown far under the media and public's radar. I examine the reasons why the president's party has done so poorly in the midterms. Most importantly, he provides a blueprint for the Democrats to reverse their often-dismal showing in the midterm elections.

The Midterms Why They Are So Important and So Ignored offers fresh insights into a part of the American political process that has meant so much to the governance of the country. But at the same time has received so little public attention and so little overall voter participation and interest. So little that it represents an embarrassing stain on our democracy.

No one knew that better and the high stakes involved in the midterm elections than Biden. In a meeting with key Democratic House members in October 2021, Biden was emphatic, "I know that I need you all to hold your seats in order for the second two years of my term to be productive."

He and every other president in the nation's history have said the same about the midterms.

1

The Tortured History of the Midterms

On November 4, 1862, President Abraham Lincoln was greatly worried. This was the date midterm elections were scheduled. As usual in the midterms, many state legislative offices and every House seat were up for grabs.

Lincoln was a Republican wartime president. And in 1862 he was waging a brutal war against the secessionist South. A war that he and the North were not winning. There was no end to the war in sight. The casualties were soaring. Untold thousands of voters in the north were souring on the war. Many in the North out and out sympathized with the Confederacy. The betting odds were that voters would take out their frustration and hostility toward Lincoln, the war, and the Republican party at the polls. They would use the midterms to send a message.

The president's party did not lose the House. But it lost

seats in Congress more than in any other year it would not have lost. One reason was there were no Southern Democrats left in Congress. If not for that, the chances were good that the Democrats might have seized Congress. As it stood, Republicans still lost more than two dozen seats in the five states that Lincoln won in 1860 (New York, Pennsylvania, Ohio, Indiana, and Illinois). Democrats grabbed two of the governorships but almost certainly would have won more if more Republican governors had been up for reelection that year.

The results were a rude wake-up call for Lincoln and the Republicans. The party officials called it a "great, sweeping revolution of public sentiment and a most serious and severe reproof." The Democrats gloated that "the verdict of the polls "was a rejection of the Republicans and their goal of vigorously pressing the war until slavery was abolished.

Lincoln for his part had his usual homespun answer to the election results. He said he felt "like a boy who stubbed his toe—too big to cry but it hurt too much to laugh."

The midterms didn't unhinge Lincoln and the Republicans from their control of Congress. Nor did it ultimately prevent them from attaining their wartime aims and winning the war. However, it was the first major midterm election that proved that the midterms could be treacherous and uncertain ground for whichever president and party held the White House.

Voters could not only turn out in numbers but use the elections as a platform to voice their displeasure at the direction of the country or outright punish the party in power. It was a lesson that nearly every president in the decades after the 1862 midterm elections would painfully learn repeatedly.

Despite their relative low-end priority in the media and public's scope throughout much of their history, the midterms have been firmly encoded in America's political tradition almost since the nation's founding. The first midterm election was held during the presidency of George Washington in 1790.

Here are the midterm gains and losses in the House and Senate for every president in the years between Washington's presidency in 1794 and Lincoln's presidency in 1862:

Year	Sitting president	President's party	Net gain/loss of president's party[1]	
			House seats	Senate seats
1790	George Washington	None[a]	+3: (37 ▶ 40)	0: (18 ▶ 18)
1794			-4: (51 ▶ 47)	+3: (16 ▶ 19)
1798	John Adams	Federalist	+3: (57 ▶ 60)	0: (22 ▶ 22)
1802	Thomas Jefferson	Democratic-Republican	+1: (38 ▶ 39)	-6: (15 ▶ 9)
1806			+2: (114 ▶ 116)	+1: (27 ▶ 28)
1810	James Madison	Democratic-Republican	+13: (94 ▶ 107)	0: (26 ▶ 26)
1814			+5: (114 ▶ 119)	-3: (26 ▶ 22)
1818	James Monroe	Democratic-Republican	+13: (145 ▶ 158)	+2: (28 ▶ 30)
1822			+34: (155 ▶ 189)	0: (44 ▶ 44)
1826	John Quincy Adams	Democratic-Republican[b]	-9: (109 ▶ 100)	-2: (21 ▶ 19)
1830	Andrew Jackson	Democratic[c]	-10: (136 ▶ 126)	+1: (25 ▶ 26)
1834			0: (143 ▶ 143)	+1: (21 ▶ 22)
1838	Martin Van Buren	Democratic	-3: (128 ▶ 125)	-7: (35 ▶ 28)
1842	John Tyler	None[d]	-69: (142 ▶ 73)	-3: (30 ▶ 27)
1846	James K. Polk	Democratic	-30: (142 ▶ 112)	+2: (33 ▶ 35)
1850	Millard Fillmore	Whig	-22: (108 ▶ 86)	-3: (36 ▶ 33)
1854	Franklin Pierce	Democratic	-75: (158 ▶ 83)	-3: (36 ▶ 33)
1858	James Buchanan	Democratic	-35: (133 ▶ 98)	-4: (32 ▶ 38)
1862	Abraham Lincoln	Republican	-23: (108 ▶ 85)	+1: (31 ▶ 32)

Source: U.S. Midterm Election Results, Wikipedia

* * * * *

The midterms are general elections held at the midpoint of a president's four-year term. They are held on the

Tuesday after the first Monday in November. Every one of the 435 House representatives is up for reelection. Usually, one out of three of the one hundred senators is also up for reelection. At the state level, most of the states hold gubernatorial elections; thirty-six in all. Mayors, thousands of city and county elected officials, and citizen-sponsored, or special interest-backed initiatives are also voted on.

Two crucial questions are repeatedly asked about the midterm elections. One is why bother having them every two years since almost always throughout their history the voter turnouts for them are always lower, in many cases far lower, than in the presidential election? The second question is if that's the case why not just roll everything over into the once every four years presidential election? The turnout is guaranteed to be much greater.

The answer to both questions strikes to the heart of the fundamental constitutional precept; namely the old checks and balances notion of the best way to ensure that the country doesn't stray into totalitarian rule or dominance by any one party or even one individual at the top. The supposed guarantee of that is that there be a sort of failsafe device to give the opposition party a chance to increase its numbers and presumably power in one or both wings of Congress.

Congress was the designated check on the executive branch. The midterms were the means the Founding Fathers chose to equalize power within the government. The other means was the imposition of two-year terms for House members.

"The House of Representatives shall be composed of Members chosen every second Year by the People of the several States, and the Electors in each State shall have the Qualifications requisite for Electors of the most numerous Branch of the State Legislature."

—U.S. Constitution, Article I, section 2, clause 1

The two-year congressional term though was a compromise. Some of the Founding Fathers argued at the constitutional convention in 1787 for one-year terms. They contended that longer terms would ensure "tyranny" since congresspersons would feel so politically secure that they could ignore the wishes of their constituents knowing they didn't have to face an immediate reelection contest. That didn't fly. It would have turned Congress into a revolving door with fresh faces coming and going at every turn. This would ensure that even less got done in Congress. Others argued for three-year terms for congresspersons.

That didn't fly either. The argument against this was that a longer-term would still equal tyranny. The two-year term stood as the compromise. As one delegate put it, "It seems proper that the representative should be in office time enough to acquire that information which is necessary to form a right judgment; but that the time should not be so long as to remove from his mind the powerful check upon his conduct." The House of Representatives Historian put it simply, "Elections would be held according to a given length of time rather than when political leaders thought they would be most likely to win."

If congresspersons were elected every four years instead of every two that would up the odds that the party in power could use the longer time to firmly establish the power of incumbency, which could give he or she an unfair advantage. The incumbent would have greater financial clout, campaign resources, and name recognition. If a House representative knew they must run every two not four years this supposedly made them more likely to stay attuned to the needs of their constituents since they knew they would be back on the ballot in a couple of years.

The Senate wasn't forgotten in the debate over term lengths and when senators should run for reelection. Though the decision was made to grant six-year terms to senators, the check and balance were that the terms for senators were staggered. Every two years one-third of the senators must run for reelection. "That's why you have a third [of the Senate] turning over, so it doesn't get too far removed from currents of public opinion," noted Sidney Milkis of the University of Virginia's Miller Center of Public Affairs.

This politically pragmatic aim didn't quite work out in practice. If anything through the decades, senators have often gotten very far "from the currents of public opinion." The Founding Fathers wanted that. They wanted one of the congressional branches to provide political stability and be a bulwark against the rule of the masses. Some even derisively called it the mob.

Congress would check the president in the scheme of government, and senators would check House representatives on legislation, and other political initiatives that smacked of swaying or bowing to the whims of the masses. The other safeguard was that a senator represents the entire state. House representatives represent districts. Depending on the size and population of the state, there could be lots of districts within the state, and thus lots of congresspersons.

What the Founders could not foresee was the monumental, outsized role of money in campaigns. This gave incumbent senators and House representatives a colossal advantage. This showed in just how many got beat in the midterms—very few. The Center for Responsive Politics charted the percent of senators and House representatives that were unseated in the midterms between 1964 and 2016. Ninety-three percent of House incumbents were reelected.

Senators did slightly worse. Eighty-two percent of them were reelected in the midterms. This lower figure for senators was misleading. In most cases, they lost to equally well-financed, and politically connected, popular, state governors or congresspersons. Or they chose to retire, and the senate seat was open. No sitting senator lost to someone who just walked into politics off the streets.

* * * * *

One president wasn't satisfied with the idea of a congressperson having to run every two years in a midterm election. President Lyndon Johnson flatly called for scrapping the two-year term in his 1966 State of the Union Address. He advocated bumping the House term up to four years. "I will ask you to make it possible for Members of the House of Representatives to work more effectively in the service of the Nation through a constitutional amendment extending the term of a congressman to 4 years, concurrent with that of the President."

Johnson's call for longer terms for congresspersons went nowhere. In part because it was buried in the mass turmoil that rocked the country in the mid-1960s over civil rights and the Vietnam War. In part because there was little public agreement with Johnson's claim that Congress wasn't getting enough done on the pressing policy and legislative issues because they were too busy campaigning and raising money to get reelected. In greater part though, Johnson's call for longer terms was rejected because the Constitution was clear on the two-term limit for congresspersons. Johnson well knew that.

The Founding Fathers in their debates over terms for House representatives were equally clear that a shuffle of parties and party control in the House every now and then was best. They considered this a healthy thing for the country.

Since Johnson's failed call, there have been scattered attempts to up the term of a House representative to four years. The last was a resolution during the 1995 Congress. However, it died a quick death.

In addition, no president since Johnson's tepid, half-hearted call for a constitutional change in terms of office, which had virtually no chance of happening, has repeated that call. The two-year term limit stood. It continues to affect for better and worse how Congress conducts its business.

The House remakes itself after each midterm election—pending bills die, committee work is shelved, and new members take their seats. Most importantly, this makes it virtually certain that the party in the White House will always have to look over its shoulder every two years and hustle like mad to grab or retain control over one or both wings of Congress.

The call for four years or longer terms for House members has an opposite argument. That's the call that instead of giving House members more time in office, give them less. The term limits for House representatives have cropped up more than a few times over the years. It arises mostly out of the public's frustration with Congress that it's not doing its job. The litany of complaints is endless-bad initiatives, inaction, corruption, too cozy with corporate special interests, or just plain dislike of what Congress represents.

The public's chronic loathe of Congress is horrifyingly evident in its approval numbers. Since 2010, Congress's best showing was a thirty-six percent approval rating. At its best, two-thirds of Americans still thought Congress was worthless. During most of the years since 2010, Congress's approval ratings averaged about eighteen percent. Or, more than four out of five Americans said thumbs down to Congress.

Here's how the public rates Congress over the past near half century:

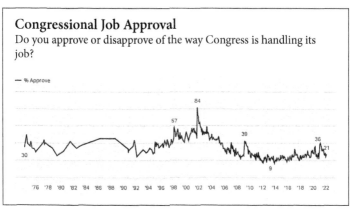

Source: Gallup

How much trust and confidence do you have at this time in the legislative branch, consisting of the U.S. Senate and House of Representatives—a great deal, a fair amount, not very much or none at all?

Great Deal	Fair amount	Not very much	None at all	No opinion
5%	32%	37%	25%	1%

Source: Gallup, Sept. 1-17, 2021

One veteran congressional watcher even compiled a checklist of the main reasons why Americans don't like and distrust Congress. Here are the top eight reasons from his list.

1. Congress exempts itself from the laws they pass like the Social Security Act and Obamacare.

2. Congress insider trades, a thing we can go to jail for by politicians who make themselves immune from prosecution.

3. Congress votes themselves pay raises.

4. Most of our representatives and senators are bought and paid for by corporations and Wall Street.

5. Congress votes for bills they do not read that affect the people but exempt themselves from.

6. No banker or Wall Street oligarch is held accountable by Congress because they pay for their reelection campaigns.

7. They vote for laws that violate the Constitution. They voted to keep the Patriot Act law against the wishes of the people.

8. It is hopelessly polarized with very little legislation of substance getting passed that both parties agree on.

It's a harsh indictment. These reasons are repeatedly cited when pollsters ask the question of why there is so much antipathy toward Congress. Yet the puzzle is why more voters don't vote senators and House members out of office when they have the chance during the midterms?

When Johnson called for extending the terms of Congress, he was aware of widespread disapproval of Congress. His answer though of tacking more years onto their terms ignored the constitutional rationale for shorter terms. There are no real constitutional arguments to be made for it. The Constitution is clear on the two-year term.

✷ ✷ ✷ ✷ ✷

There is some history, though, to the call for limits

that preceded the signing of the Constitution. Some of the colonies enacted statutes that set limits on the length of time their state representatives could serve. The delegates to the Continental Congress in 1781 were subject through the Articles of Confederation to term limits– The articles read: "no person shall be capable of being a delegate for more than three years in any term of six years."

The limits set out in the articles didn't make the final cut for the Constitution. The term limit issue would have to wait for more than two centuries for it to be raised as a significant issue again. That happened in 1990. Twenty-three states slapped term limits on their senators and House members. The limits stood for five years. It was almost certain to be challenged that the limits flew in the face of the Constitution.

In May 1995, the SCOTUS agreed and held that term limits for congresspersons were unconstitutional. The majority opinion was that term limits would lead to "a patchwork of state qualifications" for congresspersons, and that would virtually cause havoc by wiping out "the uniformity and national character that the framers sought to ensure." The ruling took painstaking care to cite the history of term limits and where things failed.

"The Articles of Confederation contained a provision for term limits. As we have noted, some members of the Convention had sought to impose term limits for Members of Congress. In addition, many States imposed term limits on state officers, four placed limits on delegates to the

Continental Congress, and several States voiced support for term limits for Members of Congress. "

Despite this widespread support, no State sought to impose any term limits on its federal representatives. Thus, a proper assessment of contemporaneous state practice provides further persuasive evidence of a general understanding that the qualifications in the Constitution were unalterable by the States."

In Federalist Papers No. 53, James Madison, a principal in the drafting of the Constitution, explained why the Constitutional Convention of 1787 rejected term limits.

"[A] few of the members of Congress will possess superior talents; will by frequent re-elections, become members of long standing; will be thoroughly masters of the public business, and perhaps not unwilling to avail themselves of those advantages. The greater the proportion of new members of Congress, and the less the information of the bulk of the members, the more apt they be to fall into the snares that may be laid before them," wrote Madison.

The SCOTUS decision was far from a clear-cut pronouncement of the inviolability of the two-term rule for congresspersons. In fact, the decision was a close-run thing. Four justices dissented. They were the conservative minority on the bench.

Justice Clarence Thomas penned an 88-page dissent, "It is ironic that the court bases today's decision on the right of the people to choose whom they please to govern them because it then invalidates a provision that won nearly 60 percent of the votes cast in a direct election and that carried every congressional district in the state." Thomas referred to an Arkansas state provision in 1992 that amended the state constitution to put term limits on officeholders including House representatives and US senators.

Thomas added, "Nothing in the Constitution deprives the people of each state of the power to prescribe eligibility requirements. . .The Constitution is simply silent on this question."

The majority decision effectively killed the scrap of the two-term rule as a legal issue. However, it did not kill it as a political issue that could be waved around from time to time. It was an issue tailor-made for use by political advocacy groups that sought to ride the wave of almost congenital public dissatisfaction with Congress. The midterms proved the ideal ground for voters to directly identify and punish those congresspersons deemed unfit for office or who provoked public anger unfit by booting them from office.

The widespread feeling among the public was that Congress needed a perpetual infusion of fresh blood. The presumption was that this would stir more energetic and creative decision-making and action, reduce corruption, and the dominance of big money special interest groups. Even then SCOTUS Justice John Paul Stevens in his majority opinion admitted that "rotation in office "could infuse fresh ideas and new perspectives and decrease the likelihood that representatives will lose touch with their constituents."

Americans Support for Establishing Term Limits for Federal Lawmakers

Suppose that on Election Day you could vote on key issues as well as candidates. Would you vote for or against a law that would limit the number of terms which members of Congress and the U.S. Senate can serve?

	Would vote "for" term limits	Would vote "against" term limits	No opinion
	%	%	%
National. adults	75	21	5
Republicans	82	15	3
Independents	79	17	4
Democrats	65	29	5
18-19 year	74	22	4
30 to 49 years	73	22	5
50 to 64 years	77	19	4
65 and older	74	21	5

Source: Gallup, Jan. 6-9, 2013

* * * * *

The most cogent argument for term limits is that it would eliminate the constant money hustle that House members must engage in to secure reelection every two years, especially during the midterms. They are marginally more vulnerable then. They often face multiple challengers. They do not have the shield of their party's president on the ballot. Again, presumably the plus from this is that more time would be spent attending to the business of Congress.

The counter to this is that the voters are still the best judge of the worth of a congressperson and they alone should decide at the polling place whether to retain or vote out a congressperson no matter how many years in office. The danger is that in making Congress a revolving door there's a constant new crop that comes in that lack the experience and the working relationships established with and between congresspersons. That takes time, even years to develop. A newcomer must start all over again in building those relationships.

There's little evidence from the states and cities that impose term limits on elected officials that limits have done much to end corruption and the money grab from special interests. Term limits would do nothing to stop the big corporate and special interest dollars flowing into the coffers of the incumbents. If anything, it makes many term-limited state legislators more likely to turn to special interests and lobbyists for information and "direction" on legislation and policy issues. This is especially true with midterm elections. They come so close on the heels of a presidential election.

While the issue of a two-year term seems legally dead, a handful of groups have kept the issue alive by lining up support from the states. They claim to have gotten fourteen states as of 2020 to pass resolutions supporting term limits. It would take thirty-eight states to ratify a constitutional change. That's a tough seemingly impossible slog. The best that can be said is that the history of electing congresspersons every two years, and thus the rationale for midterms, will always be subject to one challenge or another.

In any case, it doesn't change the reality that Congress

is repeatedly held in abysmally low esteem by a vast majority of Americans. The midterms far more than the presidential election give voters the rare chance to zero in on Congress and register their disgust by trying to oust many of them from office. If there were no midterm elections held every two years, that opportunity would be lost.

* * * * *

Since their inception during Washington's presidency, the midterms have looked a lot different in some ways than presidential elections. The presidential elections from the beginning have been the hallmark of American elections. Every president since Washington and their challengers are widely recognized among voters and have generated hot political debate and jousting.

The turnout in every presidential election has always been far greater. The last time that more voters turned out for a midterm than a presidential election was 1838. More than 70 percent of the eligible voters voted. By contrast, the turnout for the presidential election two years earlier was barely more than 50 percent.

There were two reasons for the greater turnout. There were four political parties, the Whig, the Democrat, Anti-Masonic, and the Conservative parties. Each had active constituencies, and each was grounded in the sectionalism of the states. There was a riveting issue that stirred voters. That was the nation's first major economic downturn, dubbed the panic of 1837. It was fueled by a banking crisis.

The parties furiously finger-pointed each other for the crisis. This further stimulated voter interest.

It would take more than a century later for midterm voting numbers to come anywhere close to matching the turnout for a presidential election. In the 1994 midterms, more than forty percent of eligible voters turned out. Slightly more than fifty percent turned out in the 1996 presidential election. The biggest reason for the elevated turnout then was the continuing resurgence of the GOP in the South, coupled with a martial attack by the GOP on then-Democratic President Bill Clinton.

Soon to be GOP House Speaker Newt Gingrich capsulized the conservative surge against Clinton with a big, sweeping, overblown Contract with America which was long on promise and short on delivery. But it was a good bit of political theater to crank up even more interest in the midterms that year.

Here's a comparison that shows the wide and persistent turnout gap between the midterms and the presidential elections:

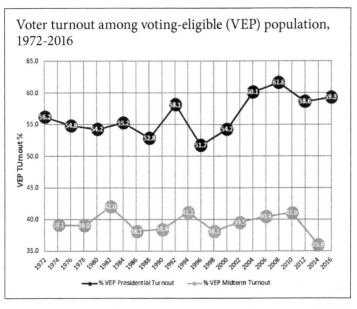

Average voting-eligible population (VEP) turnout, 1972-2016	
Presidential cycles, 1972-2016	Midterm cycles, 1974-2014
56.4%	39.3%

Source: United States Elections Project

In the first century and a half of midterms dating from Washington's presidency into the mid-1920s when women finally gained the right to vote, there was marginal voter diversity. Voters were whiter, older, male, and better educated. With the election of FDR in 1932, the pattern began to change. More Blacks, women, young people, and non-college-educated blue-collar workers turned out for both the presidential and midterm elections.

However, it didn't much alter the pattern of who consistently went to the polls during the midterms. They were still more likely to be white, male, and older voters. The age factor even more than gender and race has been the single greatest earmark of turnout for the midterms versus the presidential election. The age 45 or older group averages a whopping near sixty-five percent of midterm voters.

The older white voters, particularly in the South and the Heartland states, track hard to the GOP. It's an obvious edge that the GOP has exploited to the hilt to make gains in the midterm elections during every period in modern presidential election history when there was a Democrat in the White House.

Despite the changing voter demographics during the long history of the midterm elections, one thing has remained remarkably consistent. The president's party almost always does worse, sometimes abominably worse, in the midterms than the opposition party. The chronic lower voter turnout is one major reason for that. This largely works to the GOP's advantage. The larger turnout of older white voters that lean heavily GOP is another.

But these aren't the only explanations for why the president's party almost always suffers losses in the midterms. Other reasons reveal much that is disturbing for the American political process.

Maybe the better word is threatening.

2

The President's Party Midterm Nosedive

The worry lines seemed etched deep on the foreheads of many top Democrats in March 2022 at the winter meeting of the Democratic National Committee in Washington. The midterm elections were then eight months away and the Democrats were engaged in much hand wringing and soul searching over how to avoid the almost ritual losses in Congress and state offices that the president's party suffers in midterm elections. By any measure, the 2022 midterms would be a close contest. The Republicans needed to net less than a dozen seats to win back the House and just one seat to retake the Senate.

Vice president Kamala Harris expressed some puzzlement that things should be so hard for the Democrats in the 2022 midterms. She noted, "Our task is to show people that in many ways, they got what they ordered, right? They said this is what they wanted. They stood in line. They took time from work. It was difficult. And a lot of what they demanded, they got."

Unfortunately, it wasn't that simple. It was true the Biden administration did get much done on the economy, his judicial appointments, the battle against COVID, and other significant foreign policy and legislative initiatives were important. But the Democrats were also mindful that other presidents had also done fairly well during the first two years of their first term. Yet the opposition party still grabbed lots of seats back in the House and the Senate from the president's party, oftentimes enough to take full control of Congress. Making matters worse, at the time of the Democrats' meeting, Biden's approval ratings were in a sprint to the bottom.

The subject of why the party in the White House almost always does poorly, and sometimes colossally poor in the midterms, has been endlessly debated. One researcher even dubbed the phenomenon "historical regularity." Despite the mountain of verbiage, statistics, and speculation, there's still no single clear answer as to why that happens. Some things are known, though, about why the losses mount for the president's party during the midterms. The standard reasons offered are lower voter turnout among the president's party, voter frustration over the perceived failures even outright animosity toward the president and his party, and the relentless attacks and negative mudslinging by the party out of power against the president.

The starting point in answering why there's the ritual midterm disaster for the president and his party is the numbers. Since World War II there were only two midterm elections that the president's party gained seats. In 1994 and 2002, former President Clinton and former President Obama had the dubious distinction of having two of the biggest midterms blow out losses in history.

The Democrats lost 54 House seats in 1994 and 63 in 2010. Even the two times during the post-World War II period that the president's party didn't lose seats, the gains were minuscule. Five seats were gained in 1998 and eight seats in 2002.

Here's the chart of the president's party midterm swoon:

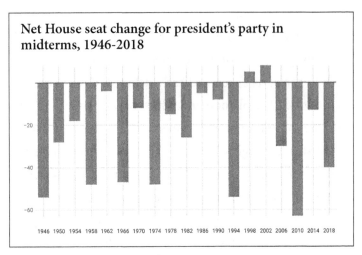

Source: Office of the Historian, House of Representatives
Created with Datawrapper
Andrew Prokop/Vox

One factor that's beyond dispute is that the party that holds the White House does a horribly poor job in motivating its supporters to turn out on midterm Election Day. While the party out of the White House works doubly hard to rev its backers up to turn out. The only exceptions to the pattern of voter falloff from the president's party were presidents Truman, Kennedy, Johnson, and Carter. Yet even they lost House seats in the midterms.

However, they got more of their party's supporters to vote. The explanation for this was that it was a different time in American politics. That was the years before 1980. There was not the sharp division and polarization between the parties and voters that have become the norm in American politics since the 1980s. Many Republican voters back then would vote for a Democrat if they felt comfortable with that Democrat's position on some of the issues. Many Democratic voters do the same and back a Republican whom they felt reflected their position on the issues.

The spirit among voters of one party willing to work with the other party characterized much of the work and relations within Congress among Democrats and Republicans in that era. Biden and former GOP senator and presidential candidate Bob Dole perhaps best epitomized that spirit of inter-party collegiality.

In February 2021, Biden paid a visit to the ailing ninety-seven-year-old Dole. They reminisced about their Senate days decades earlier. Dole called those "the good old days." He mused rhapsodically about those days, "That was a good time in our lives when we seemed to work together, and worked across the aisle, and generally got things done."

Dole sighed at the loss of those "good old days" and in one word told why things were different then than in 2021. "Trust." 'They don't trust each other." The "they" obviously was the GOP and Democrats.

The long-faded trust factor in politics that Dole lamented was savagely evident in a YouGov survey in December 2021. It found that a solid majority of Democrats flatly said that the GOP was a real danger to America. They didn't cite the usual garden variety of political differences between the GOP and Democrats. Nor did they cite the differing philosophies of the Republicans from theirs as a reason. They just said they were a danger. Most Republicans said the same thing about the Democrats. It got even nuttier.

The same month a Pew Survey found that a majority of Republicans and Democrats called the other party "immoral." Political researchers have marveled at the depth and rigidity of the polarization. They note that before 1980 it was hard to tell the parties apart. Before 1964, for instance, there were almost as many Blacks who were Republican as Democrats. The same was true for whites, Catholics, and union members.

The almost Siamese twin similarity between the parties was reflected in their platforms. The American Political Science Association back then even bemoaned that the "Alternatives between the parties are defined so badly that it is often difficult to determine what the election has decided even in broadest terms." This wasn't to say there weren't flashpoint issues before the 1980s that stirred sharp differences between and among various groups such as civil rights, immigration, the economy, armament, and so on but this didn't ram itself into the cutthroat political warfare that characterized American politics post the 1980s.

* * * * *

The first major signs of the sharpening of the political lines came in the late 1960s. Richard Nixon's shrewd play of the crime in the streets, law and order line, and his Southern strategy that downplayed civil rights deliberately played to the fears and biases of many white, blue-collar, and rural voters. Blacks by then had deserted the GOP in droves. The GOP became whiter, more male, more evangelical, and more rigidly conservative.

By the 2016 presidential election, Trump had fine-tuned all of the racial, gender, and ethnic divisive points that the GOP had fashioned since the 1980s into fine art. The only real difference between what Trump did with naked race-baiting and what legions of other GOP presidential candidates and presidents from Nixon to George W. Bush, and GOP state and local candidates and elected officials did with race was that his was blatant and in-your-face bigotry.

The others were subtle, sneaky, and loaded with emotional hot button code words and phrases that were designed to stoke the racial fires to win and maintain office. They knew that no overt mention of race was necessary to tug at the emotional strings of the GOP's core constituency—older whites, rural, and blue-collar workers. A wink and a nod with the code words on welfare cheats, entitlements, tax and spend big government, and immigrants, and the endless wedge issues from gay marriage to abortion was more than enough to boost their poll ratings.

By then polls had repeatedly shown that millions of whites were wracked with worry, edginess, and fearful about the future and the direction of the country. Many were gripped by the horrid thought of losing their numbers and power. The usual stock code words and phrases that GOP establishment politicians worked so well in the past couldn't compete with a good old-fashioned appeal to Black crime, Muslim bashing, and "send them all packing back across the border "shouts. Trump proved that permanently polarizing the parties could pay big dividends in a presidential election and, of course, the midterms.

The deliberate inflaming of political passions though cast a huge smudge on the U.S.'s long-standing reputation as the bastion of democracy. The January 6 capital insurrection, the GOP's overt and tacit endorsement of Trump's long-winded campaign to declare the 2020 elections invalid, and the legions of new GOP controlled state legislature passed laws rolling back voting rights, marked the U.S., not solely the political parties as "in danger."

In November 2021, the International Institute for Democracy and Electoral Assistance, a watchdog group, branded the U.S. among its list of "backsliding democracies." It concluded in its *Global State of Democracy Report 2021,* "The United States, the bastion of global democracy, fell victim to authoritarian tendencies itself, and was knocked down a significant number of steps on the democratic scale."

Interestingly, the U.S. had the dubious distinction of being added to the failing democracy list while countries considered authoritarian such as Ukraine and North Macedonia fell off the list. Both were considered by the Institute as more democratic than the U.S.

More than a few global leaders repeatedly agonized over the seeming grave threat that Trump posed to democratic rule in the U.S. Canada's UN ambassador Bob Rae was one. He echoed the sentiments of many diplomats when he told an interviewer in 2021 that he and others could not view the U.S. "the same way" after Trump's presidency. But it wasn't just Trump that worried the foreign watchers. Said Rae, "I don't believe the Republican Party believes in democracy."

* * * * *

As mentioned earlier, Lincoln and the Republicans worried that they'd take a beating in the 1862 midterm elections. In the years after, more presidents saw their party rack up consistent losses in the midterms. The alleged "historic regularity" of this pattern became almost a political article of faith. The Brookings Institute looked at midterm election results from that 1862 election through the midterms in Obama's second term in 2014 and found the pattern held firm. The president's party was always a big loser in those elections. It wasn't just federal elections. The losses to the party in the White House were across the board in state elections as well.

Here's an example of GOP gains in governor's races in the 2014 midterms:

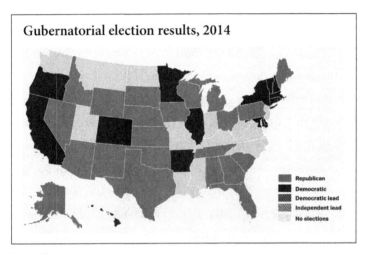

Source: Vox

* * * * *

A gauge of the success or failure of any party in any election is to figure out the best and most effective ways to turn out not only their supporters but convince a considerable number of those who have no firm party affiliation to turn out to vote as well. Further, success is attained for a party when those voters believe that it's worth not only turning out but voting for their party's candidates in state and national offices.

One explanation why the president's party has so much more difficulty in accomplishing that is that no matter how badly his party does in the midterms, he'll still be in the White House. After all, he's not on the midterm ballot. That may not be exactly a disincentive not to show up at the polls. But it's certainly not a spur to boost voter turnout. The absence of the president on the ballot then dulls the urgency of voting for many, particularly those in his party.

It's just the opposite with the party out of the White House. Their voters do have a sense of urgency for the opposition party to hit back at the administration. Thus, there is more passion and urgency in party leaders' appeals, messaging, and get-out-the-vote drives. The midterms become not the elections of the party in power to dominate. It holds the presidency.

It's the opposition party's election to try and dominate. It's even worse if the president's approval ratings in the run-up to the midterms are plunging either because of real or imagined failed policy initiatives, mediocre performance, or is the constant victim of bad press. This is always seized upon, magnified, and exploited by the opposition party.

Two examples underscore this. First are the 1994 midterm elections. The news headlines in the aftermath of the 1994 midterms with only slight variations read that then-President Clinton was drubbed in the year of the "Republican Revolution." To be charitable the Democrat's drubbing was not a revolution but a disaster for the Democrats.

The GOP grabbed the House, Senate, and most of the governorships that were on the ballot. Clinton was philosophical about the wipeout, "the American people believe, a majority of them ... that a divided government may work better than a united government." There was much truth to that based on past midterm election results. But he didn't leave it at that. He quickly added, "I disagree with that."

There was good reason for him to disagree. It was the first time since the first term of Dwight Eisenhower in the 1954 midterms that the GOP had won a majority of seats in the House. That was only one reason Clinton disagreed with the vote. He was now faced not only with a Democratic minority in Congress, but a GOP majority that was more conservative, more activist, and more anti-Clinton politically and personally. In times past when Congress was tossed back and forth between the GOP and the Democrats, there was not the extreme threat that the president's party would be throttled.

In 1994 it was different. A stacked deck GOP House and Senate did much to torpedo Clinton's agenda starting with quickly killing any push for health care reform. The GOP went for the jugular in 1998 following the Monica Lewinsky sexual cheating scandal. It impeached him and tried mightily to convict him in the Senate. The divided government that Clinton feared spelled trouble for him, and the Democrats. This was yet another product of the historic regularity of midterm woes for the president's party.

The major difference this time was that GOP House

Speaker Newt Gingrich openly boasted that he and the GOP would devise its pointed rightist program-the so-called "Contract with América"—and put sole focus on getting as much of its agenda passed. Clinton's legislative agenda was relegated to a bare afterthought.

Gingrich got so much ink, praise, and notoriety for his GOP political coup in 1994 that House Republican leaders invited him back again to advise them on how to duplicate that feat again in the 2022 midterms. When asked just what an updated "Contract with America" might look like, Gingrich ticked off a string of the GOP's most divisive, polarizing, and pet attack points, "It should be positive. School choice, teaching American history for real, abolishing the '1619 Project,' eliminating critical race theory, and what the Texas legislature is doing. We should say, 'Bring it on.'" It was to be a 1994 redux again with only the names of the characters changed.

* * * * *

Sixteen years later things got worse for the Democrats. It was the midpoint of President Obama's first term. He had only one word to describe the outcome of the 2010 midterms, "shellacking." Even that might have been too charitable a term to describe the midterm catastrophe the Democrats suffered.

He set a record of sorts. He had the dubious distinction of being the president whose party lost more seats during the 2010 and 2014 midterm elections than any other president in history. There were sixty Democratic senators in office when Obama was elected in 2008. The number plunged to forty-six by the close of his second term in 2016 There were 257 House Democrats. The number plunged to 188 when he exited the White House.

The debacle didn't stop with Congress. In both midterms, the GOP won more governorships and state legislative seats nationally. One would have to go back nearly a century to find the GOP holding the swollen number of state offices it held at the close of 2014.

The reasons for the blowout in the two midterm elections weren't hard to find. There was the traditional laxity along with widespread indifference and apathy among major segments of young, Hispanics, Blacks, and college-educated suburban women toward the election. These are the Democrats' core voters. Meanwhile, the GOP had successfully fired up its core voters, older whites, blue-collar, rural, less educated, and more evangelical whites. In any election, especially the midterms, they were far more likely to show up at the polls than minority and young voters. The GOP had another advantage the rise of a Tea Party that hectored, harassed, harangued, and virtually stalked Obama at every turn.

There was an uglier side to the GOP hit on Obama and the Democrats in the run-up to the 2010 midterms. The thought of an African American sitting in the White House was stomach-wrenching to many GOP voters. For a while, more than a few protestors at Tea Party rallies vented their spleen at Obama with outrageous, racist pictures, posters of him, and demeaning digs and taunts. To drive their racial loathing of him home they proudly waved Confederate flags. Meanwhile, millions of Americans cheered their war call and voted for the candidates that yelped it the loudest.

Obama didn't hit back. After the midterm losses he somewhat pithily chalked them up to the Democrats not thinking the midterms were "sexy enough." It was much more than that.

The Tea Party notwithstanding, it came back to the old political truism that the party out of the White House, in this case, the GOP, put a prodigious amount of time, energy, and resources into toppling Democrats in state and congressional, races. Even if Democrats had turned on the engines and put the same frenetic energy into state and congressional races and got even bigger than usual turnouts of its supporters, that still might not have staved off the midterm disasters.

In the aftermath of Obama's presidency in 2016 the GOP's base and sympathizers were now spread throughout urban, suburban, and especially rural areas in the key electoral states. The Democrats' core supporters remained overwhelmingly concentrated in the urban areas on the East and West Coasts. Democrats easily won local elections and congressional seats in districts in those states but beyond those areas, the wins for Democratic candidates become much more problematic if not nearly impossible.

GOP controlled state legislatures nationally made the

seeming impossibility worse by gerrymandering districts. This created even more politically secure districts for the GOP in several key swing states.

Here's the Red District voter spread nationally:

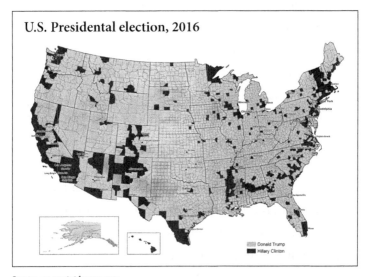

Source: www.vividmaps.com

* * * * *

The one bright spot for the Democrats was the 2018 midterm elections. They switched tables on the GOP and became the party that benefited from the president's party midterm jinx. The president this time being Trump.

Still, there was much optimism among the GOP in the run-up to that year's midterms. They seemingly held most of the winning cards. The Democrats had to defend a whopping twenty-six congressional seats. And almost half of them were in the states that Trump won on his way to the

White House in 2016. This time, though, Trump and the GOP could not buck the midterm jinx for the president's party. They managed a paltry two-seat gain. This was barely enough to keep their Senate majority rule. In the House, it was a calamity. The GOP lost almost forty seats and the Democrats took firm control.

There was no solid evidence in the months before the midterms that the Democrats had figured out how to beat Trump and the GOP in the races that they had to win to flip the House in 2018. Going into the midterms, there were three crucial tasks the Democrats had to complete to beat Trump and the GOP. The first was to understand that the GOP wouldn't beat itself. Democratic contenders would have to engage in hard, patient, organizing, telling voters why they should vote for a Democrat, and not simply vote against a Republican.

The second was to not waste time, energy, and resources on an over-the-top reach for supposed on the fence white, mostly male, less educated rural, and blue-collar workers. That wouldn't work. They were locked down for Trump and the GOP. The Democrats' task was to reconnect with and reenergize their traditional base, African Americans, Hispanics, and youth. Their voting numbers plunged in the 2016 presidential election from the 2008 and 2012 elections. The numbers plunged further in the 2010 and 2014 midterms.

The reason wasn't just that Obama wasn't on the ticket in 2016. The brutal reality was that the Democrats did what many Black voters have screamed at them about for years for allegedly doing. That is take their vote for granted.

The third task was that a party and a candidate must get off their haunches in the months before the midterm elections, put lots of face time into talking to voters about why they are important, and what exactly the candidate will do for them for their vote. Minority voters, for instance, were intently concerned about issues such as police abuse, and jobs, and what a Democrat would do about them.

Spending millions on TV ads and getting big-name celebrities or party big-shot endorsements meant little. In more cases than not, that's a turn-off. People get sick of being preached to in non-stop soundbite TV ads that endlessly go negative about the rival candidate. There's much evidence that celebrities and a national party household name official barging into a local race and commanding voters to vote for a Democrat had almost no effect.

The GOP was far from a spent party in the 2018 midterms. The Democrats had to mount a full-court press rallying their base and provide them with a clear fighting alternative program and vision to Trump and the GOP. They were largely able to do that, playing hard on fear, frustration, and animosity of and toward Trump. They turned the midterm tables on the GOP that time.

Trump, of course, saw no connection between the Democrat's big midterm gains in the House and his role in making that happen. In a Fox News interview, he airily dismissed any notion that he had some responsibility for the losses, "I have people that won't vote unless I'm on the ballot, OK?" Trump said. He continued, "My name wasn't on the ballot." When pressed that the GOP lost governorships and Senate seats in the states he won, Trump shot back, "I won the Senate, and that's historic too because if you look at presidents in the White House, it's almost never happened where you won a seat. That's a tremendous victory."

It wasn't. The Democrats' capture of the House in 2018 ensured that Trump's remaining two years in the White House would be marked by even deeper gridlock. A Democratic-controlled House would pass a blizzard of bills. A GOP-controlled Senate would in almost all cases routinely ignore them. Meanwhile, Trump had one thing in common with all past presidents that suffered the standard midterm losses for their party and subsequent loss of the party of one or both congressional chambers. He was left out in the political cold in trying to get anything of legislative substance done.

* * * * *

The historic midterm debacle for the president's party has another disturbing fall-out that extends beyond the political one-upmanship by the outlier party and its supporters. There are policy issue disagreements that go deep, arouse passions, and are ripe to be exploited to the hilt to inflame supporters. In recent decades, the list of these incendiary issues has been long: affirmative action, abortion, gay marriage, the Iraq war, terrorism, and Obamacare to name a few. They have stirred passions and anger and made it easy for the two parties to draw hard political lines in the sand against each other.

Candidates for congressional and state offices and the incumbents tug hard on the heartstrings of supporters on these issues more readily during the midterm elections when the focus is not on the White House race. The GOP prodded many supporters and fence-sitters to believe Obama was practically a card-carrying socialist. They may not have been able to get him out of the White House, but they could by making enough noise and arousing voter passions hit him hard in the political underbelly. They accomplished that by ousting as many Democrats from office as possible during the 2010 and 2014 midterms.

One other factor that has some bearing on just how good or mostly bad the president's party will fare in the midterms is the president's approval ratings. Clinton in 1998 and Bush in 2002 had super public approval ratings. Clinton for his handling of the economy which that year was booming.

Bush still basked in the glow of his perceived tough and resolute handling of the 9/11 terrorist attack. Their approval numbers were over 60 percent. Because of that, the GOP did not lose seats in the House and the Senate in the 2002 midterms. While the Democrats lost control of the House in 1998, they still managed to win seats. In the other five midterms between 1994 and 2018, the president's approval ratings hovered in the 40 percent range. That cost them heavily. Their party lost lots of seats in the midterms.

Here's the chart that shows the correlation between a president's approval rating and how his party fared in the midterms from 1994 to 2018.

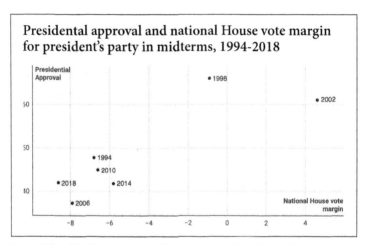

Source: Office of the Historian, House of Representatives and FiveThirtyEight
Created with Datawrapper
Andrew Prokop/Vox

Dwight Eisenhower, Richard Nixon, and Ronald Reagan (in his second term) were all popular presidents. Yet all three suffered midterm election losses to the Democrats. Politics, though, was far different then. There were many moderate Republicans and among Democrats, there were many conservatives, especially Southern Democrats. There was much more willingness of individuals to cross party lines in Congress to get things done. The reminiscing between Dole and Biden about the "good old days" typified that nostalgia among veteran politicians for the past.

Even as the political lines froze harder and harder between Republicans and Democrats by 2000, Bush Jr.'s high popularity numbers in 2002 showed that Americans, including many Democrats, still put much stock in having a tough, wartime president in the White House no matter the party label.

Bush was perceived as fitting the bill of the manly, tough-talking president, and good crisis manager. He was viewed then as a president who could best handle the terrorist threat to American security. The steady at the helm widespread public view of him rubbed off on GOP congressional candidates and incumbents in the 2002 midterms. The explanation of a sound economy boosted Clinton's standing in 1998, including with many moderate Republicans. If voters felt that their paychecks were getting bigger and that prices were not going through the ceiling, then they would be far more likely to take a benign view of the president.

Presidents wasted no time in taking the credit for the feeling among the public of economic boom times. The popular refrain has long been "it's the economy stupid." That supposedly determines whether a president will retain the White House or not. That's only true up to a point. An emotional connection between the economy's health and how individuals personally benefit from that health must be there. Voters must feel that they have more money in their pockets and are more financially secure. This feeling goes far beyond raw abstract numbers on the economy's performance.

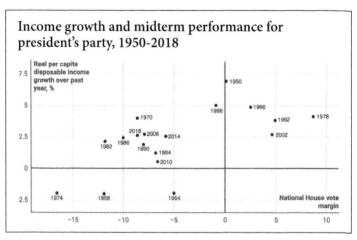

Source: Office of the Historian, House of Representatives and U.S. Bureau of Economic Analysis
Created with Datawrapper
Andrew Prokop/Vox

There's yet another curiosity about trying to predict how the president's party will do in the midterms. By their second year in office, most presidents have experienced some approval drops. They're confronted with continued and even stepped-up attacks and criticism from the other party, non-stop scrutiny by the mainstream media which harps on any presidential negatives in the handling of the issues or crises, and congressional gridlock.

This is set against the backdrop of intense political warfare over the issues that affect how the public views the president's handling of critical issues. In the eyes of many, the perception of his performance marks him as a success or failure. Many also measure his performance by whether he kept the promises he made that played a big part in convincing voters to back his White House bid.

In the run-up to the 2022 midterms, the speculation was almost nonstop over how well the Democrats would do. Biden's approval ratings were down. There were the lingering effects of the COVID pandemic. Inflation was roaring. Gas prices had soared. Biden was handicapped. There's only so much a president, any president, can do on these issues.

There are many forces far outside of their control that could break for or against a president in an election year. Even if Biden's approval ratings improved, and the Democrats worked to get their supporters to the polls, history still stood as proof that Biden's party was likely to suffer some losses. The only question was how big those losses would be?

✶ ✶ ✶ ✶ ✶

Let's fine-tune further the history of a president's party's likely fate in midterm elections. Three Democratic presidents, Truman, Clinton, and Obama suffered the greatest midterm losses in the post-World War II era. Obama as mentioned has the record. In 2010, he lost 63 House seats. Republican President Nixon suffered the greatest midterm loss in 1974. He lost 48 House seats. It wasn't hard to figure out why Obama and Nixon suffered catastrophic congressional losses those two midterm years. In 2010, the GOP attack on Obamacare had reached shrill levels.

There was not a day that passed without real and threatened court challenges, reams of angry editorials in the conservative press, and an enraged Tea Party pounding the turf round the clock against Obama and Obamacare. A wide swath of the public was divided on the issue. Many flatly bought the GOP attack line that it was too costly, too intrusive, and too much an example of big government overreach. It was still an unknown and untested measure. So, Obama with his name firmly imprinted on the legislation took all the heat, and so did the Democrats, at the midterm polls. He was stoic about it, "Some election nights are more fun than others; some are exhilarating; some are humbling."

In 1974, with Nixon, the issue was even clearer. It was Watergate. Public revulsion over Nixon's lawbreaking reached near epidemic proportions. If he had decided to hang tough against the massive public backlash and fight it out, he almost certainly would have been impeached, and quite possibly convicted in the Senate. Three months before the 1974 midterms, on August 8, 1974, Nixon did the only thing he could do to escape that fate.

He resigned under intense intra-party pressure. There was some hope that Nixon's resignation would partially do some partial damage control and avert a colossal midterm wipe-out for the GOP. That didn't happen. The GOP losses still piled up.

Eisenhower was the only other Republican President to match the 1974 midterm losses. In 1958, the GOP also lost forty-eight seats. The issue that cost the GOP seats was the economy. That year it had taken a sharp downturn.

There have been eighteen midterm elections since World War II. The president's party has averaged a loss of 26 House seats. As mentioned, FDR (1934) and Bush Jr. (2002)) saw major gains during the midterms for their respective parties. But as mentioned, FDR rode the crest of his New Deal legislation and the fever pitch backlash against the GOP for its perceived callous indifference to the dire plight of the nation's millions of poor and workers.

There's a glaring footnote to the midterm election results of these two presidents. FDR lost dozens of seats in two other midterms to the GOP during his many years in the White House. Bush rode the wave of rally around the flag patriotism and the feeling that he was a strong wartime president following the 9/11 terrorist attacks to score big in the 2002 midterms.

By 2006, things had changed. The issue was the Iraq war. It was unpopular, seemingly unwinnable, and tightly joined to Bush's presidency. His approval ratings were in a swift race to the bottom. Democrats scored big and took back control of the House and Senate. Bush was folksy in explaining the debacle, "the cumulative effect, however, was not close, it was a thumpin'."

* * * * *

One final midterm is worth looking at for past comparisons. In 1984 Ronald Reagan won a decisive reelection victory over Walter Mondale. Reagan's party didn't suffer losses in the 1986 midterms. However, the Democrats did gain House seats. The setback was far greater for Reagan in the Senate. The Democrats took it back.

Reagan played the fear card to try to stave off the loss when he flatly declared the choice was "whether to hand the government back to the liberals or to move forward with the conservative agenda into the 1990s." His plea fell flat.

Returning to the 2006 midterm blow-out for Bush, there was one major takeaway from that that can be applied to the 2022 midterms and indeed, just about any other midterm election. Then Democratic Congressional Campaign Committee Chairman, Rahm Emanuel, was direct in explaining the Democrat's big win, "Iraq was the driving factor behind everything. And October [2006] was a disastrous month [in Iraq]."

The Depression, the Korean War, the Vietnam War, Watergate, soaring inflation, high unemployment, and the list goes on and on of crisis issues that presidents have had to grapple with in their first terms. When those issues hang heavy as issues in the midterms, the president's party not only will lose but, in many cases, lose big. In 2006, as Emanuel correctly said, the issue was the increasing unpopularity of the Iraq War. That badly hurt Bush and the GOP. Unfortunately, there's only so much a president can do to get out front or avoid the prickly issues that can hurt and hurt badly the president's image. These issues are the pitfalls that can dampen his voter approval ratings.

Every president has understood and feared that disastrous happening. Trying to do damage control in the immediate months before a midterm election presents a horrid, nerve-wracking challenge for a president and his party's officials.

At a July 21 meeting with Democratic city officials, Biden took special pains to buttonhole then New York Mayoral candidate Eric Adams. Adams was a former ranking NYPD official. Biden saw his former cop credentials as particularly useful during the midterm campaign, telling him straight out that he needed him during the midterms. Adams aimed to please, "I'm going to work my ass off," the ex-cop and soon-to-be New York City Mayor eagerly said.

Biden's plea to Adams for help in the midterms was yet another troubling sign of the challenge Biden and the Democrats faced in 2022.

.

.

3

The GOP's Midterm Bullseye

Seven months before the scheduled November 2022 midterms, these headlines appeared in five different publications:

"Why Republicans Are likely to Win the 2022 Mid-Term Election"
"Republicans May Win Not Just House but also Senate in Midterm...."
"Biden Is Handing the Midterms to the GOP"
"Obama Insists Worried Dems Should Just Tell Their 'Story' to..."
"Historic Win Shows Just How Much Trouble Dems Are in for Midterms"

These headlines were just the tip of the iceberg on the headlines regarding the midterms. There were at least a dozen other publications that screamed similar headlines in the months before the midterm elections. The steady media message was that the election—then still months away—was practically over and that Biden and the Democrats would suffer a crushing midterm defeat. The much talked of "red wave" supposedly would cost the party many Senate and House seats. The Democrats almost certainly would lose control of the House or Senate or both.

There was a spate of other articles that doubledowned on this theme. They painted all kinds of doom and gloom scenarios for Biden and the Democrats supposedly when not if, the GOP took back Congress. The doomsday predictions had a life of their own and set off near panic among Biden and the Democrats. There were grim warnings and loud exhortations among state, local, and national Democratic groups to double and triple down on efforts to impress Democratic supporters and sympathizers on the danger of the loss of Congress to the GOP. It was a matter of extreme urgency for the Democrats to get the maximum turnout of their supporters in the midterms.

Scores of House Democratic party incumbents up for reelection in swing states in the 2022 midterms implored Biden to be more visible and aggressive in selling the Democrat's achievements. They wanted him to hit the road and especially turn up in their districts. Michigan Democrat Dan Kildee was one of those Democrats. He flatly told Biden, "It makes a difference when you get out there." Biden didn't push back. However, he didn't rush to the highways either.

The implicit message from the press and political pundits that prophesized disaster for the Democrats in the midterms was that the GOP was better than the Democrats in getting its people to the polls. The record for the midterms since the mid-1980s did show that the Republicans had repeatedly bested the Democrats in the midterms.

The problem was not simply turnout, but who turned out.

* * * * *

The Census Bureau's *Current Population Survey, November Voting and Registration Supplement* that was taken in March 2021 provided the most comprehensive answer to that issue. The Bureau asked several questions about voting and registration. The survey confirmed again that older, less educated, whites were more likely to vote than any other voter group. While the percentage of whites who make up the overall electorate dropped considerably since 1986 from making up 85 percent of the electorate to roughly 72 percent in 2020, they still made up the substantial majority of the nation's overall voters.

The voter demographics were just one part of the answer to who votes and why the GOP has had more success generally in the midterms than the Democrats. Older whites, those over age 50, are far more likely to vote than younger voters under age 35 in all elections.

There was more. Even the percentage difference between old and young is misleading. Midterm elections are hardest fought in these five or six key swing states, Wisconsin, Michigan, Pennsylvania, Florida, North Carolina, and Ohio. The percentage of older white, rural, blue-collar, workers without a college degree was much higher overall in those states.

They represent more than just the GOP's prime base. Their loyalty to the GOP extends back years even generations in their families. It makes no difference who the Republican candidate or incumbent is for an office or even what the office is. They reflexively vote him or her.

Their fierce loyalty to the GOP was terrifyingly evident in the immediate aftermath of the January 6 Capitol insurrection. Many House and Senate Republicans were apoplectic with rage and anger at the rioters. They blamed Trump for it. They condemned him in the strongest language for his lawlessness and criminality in inciting the rioters. But almost all of them caved and voted against the Democratic House sponsored impeachment resolution in January 2021. Only ten Republican House members broke ranks and voted to impeach Trump. GOP Senators were no better. Only seven GOP senators voted to convict him.

The reason for the GOP's political cowardice in nailing Trump was simple. They feared the wrath of and backlash from GOP voters. Ohio GOP congressman Bill Johnson was one of the Republican House members who heaped scorn on Trump for the riot. He was not among the ten who voted to impeach him. He explained why to an interviewer: "The seventy-four million people that voted for him, including the over two hundred and fifty some thousand in my district when I suggest to them there's some accountability to be shared here, man-they go ballistic. I'm just telling you that that's the kind of thing that we're dealing with, with our base." He faced serious political peril if he angered GOP voters in his district by acting against Trump. As he put it," there's the fire raging out there."

Johnson avoided drawing fire from the fevered GOP voters in his district by voting against impeachment. It was a far different story for the ten Republicans who broke ranks and voted to impeach. They were hectored, harassed, and harangued. Legions of Republican state and county organizations passed angry resolutions denouncing them. The ten political heretics heard the loud clatter against them. In the months after the impeachment vote, they lapsed into deafening silence about their vote. They were mute on any further criticism of Trump.

More than any other major Republican leader, Utah Senator Mitt Romney had spoken out loudest against Trump's outrages. He voted twice against him in the impeachment ordeals. That made him a special target of Trump. The venom spewed against him was so strong that it was reported that he took to wearing a hat to avoid recognition when he traveled for fear of being accosted by Trump backers.

McConnell also continued to aid and abet Trump. In

February 2021, barely weeks after the Trump ignited Capitol riot, he gave an interview to *Fox News*. McConnell apparently forgot that during and immediately after the riot, he had slammed Trump hard and vowed that he wanted him purged forever from American political life. When asked whether he'd back Trump for a presidential run in 2024, McConnell didn't hesitate, "the nominee of the party? Absolutely."

Here's the voter turnout rates by race and ethnicity since 1984 that gives another answer as to why the groveling to Trump:

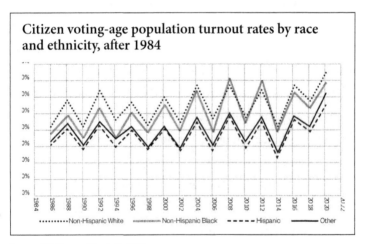

Source: U.S. Census, March 17, 2020

There were ten midterm elections between 1978 and 2014. With few exceptions, the GOP turned out far more of its supporters than the Democrats. The average overall GOP turnout has been three points better than that for the

Democrats. At first glance, this may not seem a lot. However, in close races in swing-state districts that 3-point edge can and often does spell the difference between victory and defeat, mostly defeat for the Democratic incumbent or candidate.

It makes an enormous difference to many voters who's in the White House. If it's a Democrat, the chances are much greater that the small point edge for the GOP looms even larger. The reverse is the case if the White House occupant is a Republican. It comes back to the GOP's greater ability to turn on the burners in prodding its base to turnout during the midterms. The crucial factor again is loyalty and identification. GOP voters stubbornly identify much more closely with their party than Democratic voters do with their party.

Here's the breakdown on the Republican midterm turnout advantage:

	A closer look at the Republican midterm turnout advantage	
The shift toward the GOP in party identification margin from all registered voters to those who voted in the midterm election		
	Republican Midterm Turnout Advantage	
	Under a Democratic President	Under a GOP President
1978 (Carter)	+6	—
1982 (Reagan)	—	+1
1986 (Reagan)	—	None
1990 (H.W. Bush)	—	+3
1994 (Clinton)	+6	—
1998 (Clinton)	+3	—
2002 (W. Bush)	—	+2
2006 (W. Bush)	—	None
2010 (Obama)	+6	—
2014 (Obama)	+5	—
Average	+5	+1
Median	+6	+1
Turnout is self-reported for 1982, 1994, 1998 and 2002. Turnout is from verified voter files for all other years.		

Source: American National Election Studies, Cooperative Congressional Election Study

* * * * *

The 2018 midterms were a rare exception. Trump's overall ratings tracked low during the entirety of his first two years in office. At the same time, the Democrats' fervent hopes and even predictions that they would make the midterms a blue wave and take back the House and maybe even the Senate became a reality. Their hope was based on several valid notions.

One was that women, Blacks, Hispanics, and young persons were so furious at Trump and the GOP that they'd storm the polls in November 2018 in the couple of dozen up for grabs contested congressional districts. The Democrats hoped that swell of voters would be more than enough to tip those districts to the Democrats.

The white-hot battle over Brett Kavanaugh's SCOTUS confirmation, and the insults heaped on women who told their harrowing stories of sexual abuse, did much to seal the midterm election fate of the GOP. There was robust evidence that there was much Democratic anger at Trump, and that more Democratic voters would turn out on Election Day.

The stakes in 2018 in some ways were even greater than the 2016 presidential election for Democrats. They had two years of Trump attacks, name-calling, hard rightist, and racist pandering under their belts. Their worst nightmare about Trump had come true. Many Democratic voters knew that.

The Democrats mounted intense voter registration drives. In addition, a massive amount of small-donor donations poured into Democratic candidate's coffers. Top Democrats finally took off the gloves and urged Democratic candidates to get down and dirty with Trump and the GOP. They hit back hard at his smears and lies. These were good signs that Democrats understood that the 2018 midterm election would tell much about the immediate future direction of the country.

Trump and the GOP understood that too. They also worked overtime to stymie any Democratic surge in that year's midterms. Trump reached back into his stockpile of racist, inflammatory, incendiary, and scare rhetoric and tactics from name-calling immigrants to loudly heaping praise on a thuggish congressperson who body-slammed a reporter.

Then he piled that on with a hysterical trash of anyone who voted for a Democrat as "crazy." This stuff worked to an extent in 2016 with many frustrated, angry, and fearful non-college-educated, blue-collar, and rural white males, in the handful of must-win states. Trump hoped it would work again.

It wasn't just Trump dropping his usual incendiary bombshells to whip up GOP voter mania ahead of that year's midterms. The GOP dug deep into its bag of dirty tricks pulling out all stops to damp down the vote. The most outrageous ploy was in Georgia where it scrubbed tens of thousands of mostly Black voters from the voting lists on the flimsiest of excuses. However, there were variations of the GOP's vote suppression shenanigans in other states.

The GOP didn't stop there. It went even lower in the gutter and dredged up a phony, front group called "Black Americans for the President's Agenda." It bankrolled a series of insanely ludicrous radio ads screaming that a vote for the Democrats would lead to "lynching" Blacks in a few states. This was on top of the usual king's ransom of cash that GOP affiliated PACS, the Koch Brothers, and other major right-wing corporate donors plowed into GOP campaigns nationally.

Trump played one other card. He finger-pointed the GOP for losing the House—not himself- even before one midterm vote had even been counted. This was less a dodge of the blame for the GOP's losses than an effort to whipsaw the GOP and his base to even greater heights or depths to beg, borrow or steal the election and ward off any defeat.

Trump and the GOP banked that this was more than enough to continue to fuel media talk and Democratic doubts about the outcome of the midterms. The great horror of the GOP was that a Democratic surge would stop the GOP dead in its tracks in its drive for total domination of national and state governments in the country, not just now but for years to come.

The GOP gambit to prevent a 2018 midterm GOP reversal in congressional and state offices was to talk and write a lot about a blue wave trickle rather than a flood sweeping over the country that midterm election. That fits neatly into the GOP's aim to do and say anything that would keep as many Democratic base voters as possible away from the polls. If that had happened it would have continued the historic pattern of the GOP out organizing, out strategizing, and outmaneuvering the Democrats to ensure a bigger and more spirited turnout of its supporters in that year's midterms. 2018 was one of the rare times that didn't happen.

* * * * *

Four years later the political landscape seemingly had changed for the 2022 midterms. Trump was out. The Democrats clung to a bare majority in the Senate and a less than a commanding majority in the House. As mentioned, many GOP strategists, a bevy of pundits, and some polls were practically declaring it a foregone conclusion that the GOP would win big and would likely win one if not both congressional chambers.

This was in part based on the usual GOP well-oiled, and proven machine for mobilizing its supporters and getting them to the polls. It was an off-year election with the president not on the ballot. Biden had tanking approval ratings. There was the historic propensity of the president's party to do lousy in the midterms.

That wasn't all. The GOP openly said it had a virtual can't lose strategy for ensuring that it came out on top in the midterms again. That was simply picking a handful of issues that the public was disenchanted with Biden on. The four that topped the list were the public's continued worry over COVID, soaring gas prices and inflation, and much anger at getting the U.S. totally out of Afghanistan with all the chaos that engendered. Then there was the GOP's perennial bread and butter issue, the crime scare.

The GOP also had the marvelous, well-honed capacity to take cultural, wedge issues such as critical race theory and transgenderism and squeeze them for all their emotional and fear-mongering worth. This created and then heightened fears, anxieties, and anger. The GOP understood that elections were as much about emotions, as the issues, and to be able to tap those raw public feelings translated into voter surges at the polls.

National Republican Congressional Committee communications director Michael McAdams was blunt, "If Republicans had a significant advantage on handling the issue of rising prices, rising crime, or the crisis on the southern border, we'd be in good shape. The fact that we have an advantage on all three means electoral disaster for vulnerable Democrats."

There was more still. A great debate raged over the mostly manufactured clamor over critical race theory. It was allegedly being crammed down students' throats in school districts around the country. The GOP claimed that in almost all cases the cramming was done by Democratic politicians and liberal Democratic school district officials. The issue seemed tailor-made to boil the blood of GOP backers.

Republican strategist Ford O'Connell pulled no punches in telling how the GOP could make use of the issue to inflame, "This is an issue that can really help Republicans win back those suburbs that they might have lost in the 2020 election. It could contribute to a red wave in 2022, particularly as it relates to the House of Representatives."

Democrats weren't caught flat-footed on this potential GOP culture war issue. The word from most Democratic operatives was to not fall for the ploy and engage in meaningless debate over it, Instead, Democratic congressional candidates and incumbents should stay focused on vital issues such as health, education, the economy, and ways the Democrats fight to improve them.

Emotions and fears have long been the twin tools to build a winning campaign in American politics. GOP presidents turned it into practically a state-of-the-art endeavor. There was Nixon's law and order, and silent majority pitch. There was Reagan's evil empire Soviet tag. There were Bush Sr's Willie Horton crime fear ads. There was Bush Jr's hyper-exploit of the terrorism fear. GOP strategists have played hard along the way on abortion, gay rights, gay marriage, affirmative action, and assorted other culture war and diversionary issues. They have proven often effective tacts to stoke voter passions.

Trump took the fear factor endemic in politics to new heights of absurdity. He tried to turn the 2020 presidential campaign into the dirtiest, vilest, non-stop attack leaden campaign in U.S. history. He hurled every insult he could think of at Biden and Vice-presidential candidate Harris. As noted, some of that vitriol had spilled over into the 2018 midterms.

✷ ✷ ✷ ✷ ✷

There was much more to the Trump victory game plan than the standard schoolyard name-calling and finger-pointing. He tipped the first one with his talk to the

GOP-aligned Council for National Policy in August 2020. He blasted Biden for making what he called Democratic-run cites unsafe.

In the days after, he forcefully snatched a page from the 1968 presidential campaign playbook of Richard Nixon. He railed that he would be the arch defender of America's alleged beleaguered, disrespected, and under siege police. He ripped the demands to defund and, even more, terrifying to some, abolish the police. He conjured up the image of Black Lives Matter as a nihilistic, anti-white, anti-police, lawless group. He made the law and order sell to nervous, fearful voters in the swing states, and right-leaning independents. They were the ones Trump again counted on to tip the scales in the crucial swing states in his direction.

He relentlessly tossed the standard conservative smear of Biden and the Democrats as tax and spend, liberal big-government proponents out. He had the perfect foil in House Speaker Nancy Pelosi and the Democratic-controlled House's seeming gargantuan COVID stimulus recovery spending plans. This openly and subtly fueled a large segment of middle- and working-class workers' disdain for liberal solutions to problems.

In 2016 nearly everyone wrote Trump off as a certain loser to Hillary Clinton. That was a mistake. There was always a path for Trump and the GOP to win no matter how terrible things appeared on the surface for him. The path is the one that continually surfaces in midterm elections that the GOP uses to its great advantage. The reliability of older whites, and less educated, blue-collar, and rural whites in the electorate to push GOP candidates over the top. Elections are almost always won by candidates with a solid and impassioned core of bloc voters who vote. Older whites fit that template in a far greater number and percentage of voters in comparison to Hispanics and Blacks, and especially young voters in the midterms.

Ohio Congressman Johnson characterized the ferocity of millions of fanatic Trump and GOP backers as the "raging fire." GOP candidates and incumbents could not risk being singed by it.

The GOP intended to stoke that fire into a red-hot flame for the 2022 midterms.

4

Culture Wars, Vote Suppression, and Messaging

"Watch, watch, watch! Those are my people." The usual boastful Trump in a phone call to South Carolina senator Lindsey Graham took full credit for tipping the governor's race in Virginia in November 2021 to GOP candidate Glenn Youngkin. Trump's braggadocio notwithstanding, he may have been accurate in his estimate of himself and as he put it "my people" to provide the margin of victory in an election.

Trump's command emphatically demonstrated that his White House loss in 2020 did not affect the seemingly inherent edge the GOP had over the Democrats in midterm and off year elections. That combined with the fear and emotion factor were still powerful weapons the GOP and Trump was well prepared to employ for the 2022 midterms.

The down-ballot election results in the 2020 presidential election were proof of that. The huge gains that the Democrats had made in electing many fresh Democratic faces in the House in the 2018 midterms were almost wiped out even in the wake of Trump's defeat. The numbers loss represented a near-total reversal of Democratic gains from 2018. The Democrats gained fourteen new seats in 2018. They lost twelve of them in 2020.

Alexander Burns and Jonathan Martin in *This Will Not Pass Trump, Biden, and the Battle for America's Future,* noted, "It was a wrenching reversal for Democrats and a sign that a national electorate that repudiated Trump still harbored serious misgivings about the liberal opposition party."

This was a delicate way of saying that GOP House and Senate candidates and incumbents made no inroad with GOP core voters, non-college-educated, rural, and blue-collar workers, and even many suburban voters. Steve Scalise, a top GOP House member," giddily observed that the GOP's resurgence in congressional races in the 2022 presidential election proved "that the GOP strategy of demonizing Democrats as cop-hating communists had worked."

Scalise's over-the-top hyperbole notwithstanding, he wasn't too far off in his cynical assessment of how the GOP whittled away at the Democrat's congressional bulge, at least with Trumps still colossal number of backers in Trump country regions.

Democratic National Committee Chair Jaimie Harrison fingered the game plan the GOP would again try to put to devastating use in the 2022 midterms, "It is a party built on fraud, fear, and fascism." During the SCOTUS confirmation hearings for Ketanji Brown Jackson, as mentioned, the GOP senators on the Senate Judiciary Committee put the fear and emotional factor on grotesque display. They hectored Jackson on critical race theory, transgenderism, and other issues that had absolutely nothing to do with judicial philosophy or her past judicial record.

This was nothing more than a rehash and update of the old cultural wars the GOP waged in the 1990s and during Obama's presidency to arouse GOP voters. The ploy then was to hammer the Democrats on their support of gay rights and in particular gay marriage. That played well with a major segment of the GOP's voter base, conservative Christian evangelicals.

The 2022 variant of that was to dredge up and harp heavily on the issue of gender identity to stir passions. The GOP controlled Florida legislature for instance in March 2022 passed the Parental Rights in Education bill popularly branded a "don't say gay" legislation that forbade teaching about sexual orientation or gender identity.

GOP legislators in nearly two dozen other states quickly picked up on the Florida measure and rushed to put a similar law on the books, "The truth is, this has never been about Florida," said Brandon Wolf, the press secretary for the LGBTQ advocacy group Equality Florida, "It's never been about one state but rather a policy objective from the furthest right-wing of the Republican Party to try to roll back civil liberties and progress through fear and manipulation of their base."

The bills were torn straight out of the GOP playbook from the 1990s. Then the issue was gay rights and gay marriage prohibitions. There was a spate of bills and ballot initiatives that popped up in several states during that period clamping bans on gay marriage and defining marriage as solely between a man and a woman. Most of the laws were eventually struck down and the SCOTUS eventually made the issue moot by upholding gay marriage. Yet the enduring impact of this one cultural war issue was still very much evident. Four states still had anti-gay bans on their books in 2022.

The number of individuals that identify as transgender is infinitely minuscule to the general population. However, it's not the numbers that the GOP was concerned with but using the issue to inflame and get out its voters. It's no accident that the issue became a flashpoint issue after Biden's presidential election and in the months before the 2022 midterms.

Timing in politics is everything. Here are the numbers. Twenty-two of the sixty anti-LGBTQ proposed bills in 2019, or 37 percent, were anti-transgender bills, compared with 153, or 80 percent, of 191 anti-LGBTQ bills in 2021. By March 2022, sixty-five percent of the anti-LGBTQ bills targeted transgender people.

This was an issue the GOP regarded as one that

packed just enough punch to polarize and stir voter passions. The target was GOP supporters and anyone else who had qualms about transgenderism and gays. They were the ones deemed most susceptible to the anti-transgender slurs.

Florida Senator Rick Scott, 2022 National Republican Senatorial Committee chair, wasted no time in jumping on the issue with the avowed goal of using it to take back the Senate for the GOP in the 2022 midterms. His committee made that plain in a document it issued in February 2022. It pledged to rigidly draw the federal government line on what is and isn't worthy of gender protection. Said the document "Humans are born male and female, there are two genders, and to deny that is to deny science."

Scott promised that a GOP-controlled Senate would make sure there or no requirements to answer questions about "gender identity" or "sexual preference." Scott said the ban would be sweeping—doctors, sports teams, and employers would not be put to any test on discrimination on the issue of transgenderism.

A *Harvard CAPS/Harris* poll in November 2021 provided Scott and the GOP a lot of grist for its attack. Most voters agreed that "people are born with their gender." Scott had another weapon in the GOP's crass midterm manipulation of the issue. That was Trump.

He poked fun at and ridiculed a University of Pennsylvania transgender swimmer to a packed cheering crowd in Texas. He spoke the month before Scott's Senate midterm election committee boasted it would be the defender of sexual separation. GOP candidates and incumbents battling for a congressional seat in the midterms took the cue and either backed anti-transgender legislation or tried to scrap whatever protections had already been put on the books.

Terry Schilling, the president of the pro-family American Principles Project, best summed up the GOP's cynical midterm campaign move, "This is exactly the type of platform GOP candidates should be running on this year. This is how the GOP will win elections, not by surrendering the culture war but by fighting back."

* * * * *

By far, though, the GOP padded its slight point advantage in voter turnout over the Democrats in midterms by a continued pulsating attack on alleged voter fraud. The aim has been to further shove down the number of potential Democrats that show up at the polls during the midterms

Voter suppression is a well-documented fact in American politics. The GOP has welded it as a potent weapon to assure its continued domination of American politics in the general election and especially the midterm elections The even more terrifying reality is that vote suppression has the force of law behind it. GOP-controlled legislatures can ram through legislation that allows the secretary of states to legally make the call about which votes can and can't be counted.

The lawsuits that are filed against this blatant vote suppression are at best stop-gap efforts to blunt some of the damage. They do little to change the legal authority states have to make the call about the voting process.

The vote suppression ploys the GOP have employed in a variety of states since 2010 include closing polling places, limiting voting hours, a rigid requirement for ID, and outright purging voters from the rolls if they haven't voted in a recent election. These actions were all upheld by various courts including the Supreme Court.

Court challenges against the other GOP voter suppression ploy of tightly gerrymandering districts to make it impregnable to a Democratic contender have failed. These restrictions imposed on the voting process by GOP governors and GOP-controlled legislatures particularly in Florida and Ohio, the two states that virtually determine who sit in the Oval Office, heighten the danger to Democrats in both the general election and the midterms.

Here's the state's scorecard on voter suppression in the U.S. since 2011:

Source: Brennan Center for Justice

Trying to challenge the legality of voter suppression, though, is a tough nut to crack. The GOP's caustic, but stupendously successful assault on the landmark 1965 Voting Rights Act over the years made voter suppression challenges hard to win. More on this later.

The GOP kicked voter suppression into high gear after Obama's White House win in 2008. It continued to peck away at eroding the Act with the rash of photo identification laws that GOP governors and GOP controlled state legislatures enacted.

The Democratic-controlled House in 2021 passed a series of democratic reforms to break the stifling grip of GOP voter suppression hijinks. A centerpiece was automatic voter registration which would automatically add eligible voters to the rolls. The democracy reforms as expected languished in the Senate with GOP senators simply agreeing to do nothing on the bill.

The GOP stall along with the intense pressure from the Congressional Black Caucus, civil rights leaders, and House Speaker Nancy Pelosi to act on the bill frustrated Biden. In a speech in Tulsa in June 2021, he acknowledged that he had heard the criticism from many quarters about nothing being done by him to help get a voting rights bill passed. The reason was simple. He didn't have the votes. Biden was specific about the voting math in Congress saying that he only had "a majority of effectively four votes in the House and a tie in the Senate. "

The absence of a bill that restored at the federal level some semblance of voter equity merely ensured that the Democrats would continue to have even fewer potential Democratic voters on midterm Election Day than the GOP.

* * * * *

In politics more than anywhere else in life the medium is the message. The GOP's most pernicious and insidious voter suppression and fear-mongering ploys could be partially overcome by delivering the right message to Democratic voters that spurred them to vote. Biden, Obama, and many Democrats were aware of the crucial role that messaging played in driving voter turnout.

They voiced concern continually in the months before the 2022 midterms that the Democrats were failing to effectively message their accomplishments. Biden and Obama were right to criticize. Each had compelling issues to message before the midterms in their first two years in the White House. Obama secured the passage of the Affordable Care Act in 2010. All GOP efforts to scuttle it had failed. The Act became enormously popular over the years.

Biden got his signature $1.9 trillion American Rescue Plan passed in March 2021. This included an expanded child tax credit as well as money for vaccines and small businesses. These were extremely popular measures. The polls bore this out. They boosted Biden's approval rating in March 2021 to over 60 percent.

The high public approval of the ACA and the Rescue Plan was fine but meant little in an election year unless the message of their importance and benefit resonated with voters. Biden recognized the problem was not his outstanding legislative accomplishments. It was how many voters understood at the gut level the good that these measures did for them. As noted, Biden heard the loud clamor from many Democrats to hit the midterm campaign trail and sell the party and Biden's agenda to many increasingly skeptical voters.

This is where the crucial importance of delivering the right message came in with a vengeance. One year after the legislation passed, Biden's approval rating was in a mad dash to the bottom. There was a drop of more than twenty percentage points. By then the measures that he got passed had benefited millions of Americans. So, what happened to make him suddenly so unpopular with so many of those same people who continued to benefit from his legislation?

One easy answer was that a lot of people didn't like Biden's abrupt withdrawal from Afghanistan in August 2021. However, the withdrawal was not Biden's doing. GOP President Trump brokered the withdrawal long before Biden took office. Another easy answer was that a lot of people were mad and blamed Biden for the huge spike in gas prices and inflation.

However, gas and oil prices are established near structural cyclical and recurring economic and financial problems that a president has almost no control over. The gas price rise of early 2022 was a prime example of this. Biden repeatedly denounced the price jumps, offered to make lots of oil available from America's domestic supplies, and even saber rattled OPEC about the price jumps. Yet the message didn't come through too many that Biden meant business and that some action would follow from this. To many, it seemed nothing more than talk, and more talk.

There was a tie-in of rising oil prices to the midterms. Four decades plus earlier during the presidency of Jimmy Carter, gas prices took an extreme price leap in the months immediately before the 1978 midterms. The GOP gained three seats in the Senate and fifteen seats in the House. By midterm standards, these were not punishing losses for the Democrats. They still retained control of Congress. But the results did give a warning that voters were keenly attuned to economic issues. Even more ominously it signaled the start of many voters' march to the right. The march exploded in the Reagan Revolution two years later.

* * * * *

One key to delivering a message that touches a nerve and makes a president look like he's a man of real action is to keep the message and the wording punchy and simple. If it's perceived as complicated, abstract, or even non-existent, it falls flat. The GOP has long understood that. Nixon's "crime in the streets," Reagan's "Morning in America," Bush Jr.'s "Mission Accomplished," Trump's "shut the border down," and "Make America Great Again," were perfect examples. They might seem facile, even inane, but in the arena of high-stakes politics, they worked because they were simple and understandable.

The other key is to frame the message in a way that touches an emotional chord with the average voter. If that voter is a less educated, white rural, or blue-collar worker, and an evangelical in the South or the Heartland states, that's almost certainly a surefire winner. These are the votes that form a big segment of the GOP's base. Those campaign throw-away lines from the four GOP presidents touched a nerve with them.

The Democrats by contrast have been great at churning out phenomenal, detailed position papers and tracts on the issues. In presidential and midterm campaigns, their websites have brimmed with stats, charts, and detailed information about everything from the economy to foreign policy issues. They were mostly unread and had no unifying, memorable catchphrase, or compact emotion-charged message, which could be spun out and repeated over and over to the public and that would stick.

One commentator cited Biden's slogan and legislative initiative, "Build Back Better" as a near textbook example of this. It was compact, but it didn't say anything. He quipped, "It sounds like a chain of chiropractors." Contrast that with Trump's "Make America Great Again" chant. That punched the narcissistic, narrow, cheerleading, we're going to be back on the top again, button for millions.

Biden's failure to message effectively his administration's accomplishments so worried Biden's top pollster, John Anzalone, that he addressed an urgent memo to his boss in June 2021. He had conducted a series of focus groups among swing-state voters and found that voters there were not cheering Biden for his attempt to pass a massive infrastructure bill that would create jobs and promote economic recovery. Instead, they were hand-wringing over inflation and crime.

Anzalone drew the obvious conclusion: "Republican leaders are likely to attempt to ratchet up attacks and tie national Democrats to the trend." Anzalone made clear in the memo that Biden could counter by simplifying his message, dropping the infrastructure verbiage, and calling it the more emotion boosting "the jobs bill."

* * * * *

With time running out before the 2022 midterms, and the warning bells sounding louder about pending disaster, the Democrats pivoted in their messaging. "Build Back Better" was pushed to the curbside, and slogans like "the Democrats put checks in the pocket," and "are bringing jobs back now" became the pitches. They sounded suspiciously like they were striking a Trumpian note in compact, stick point messaging.

The object was to better sell the idea to voters that Biden's economic agenda was working and had helped lots of people. It didn't wipe away the discontent and anger millions of voters had about inflation and high gas prices, but at least the message was simple, intelligible, and posed a counter to the economic fears whipped up by the GOP. It was a classic case of trying to beat the GOP at its own game. The Democrats' sole goal was to spur more Democratic voters to the polls in the 2022 midterms.

As the clock wound down to the November 2022 midterms, an increasingly frustrated Biden in the latter part of April 2022 voiced several complaints about the Democrats get out the vote efforts. He started with himself. He said he was having a tough time getting out of the White House with all the issues and problems piled on his table to deal with. Biden was convinced that with greater visibility and public contact he could better message and sell his agenda to more voters.

A couple of Biden's advisors put it this way, "Part of the value of contrast in any midterms is to try to force voters to think about this as a choice, as opposed to making it a referendum. That's most effectively done from the top – it's hard to send candidates around the country even if they're all singing from the same hymnbook if you don't have the President driving it."

Another complaint, though veiled, Biden had was over the lackluster or non-existent efforts of some top Democrats to tout his agenda to voters. He again called on them to hit hard on the theme that if Democrats lost one or more of the wings of Congress "think of the grim alternative."

Finally, Biden lambasted the never-ending speculation that he might not run for reelection in 2024. He made clear again that he would run. But he also saw this as a distraction that took the focus away from Democrats doing their job which was to put maximum effort into getting a big voter turnout in the midterms.

There indeed was no alternative if Democrats wanted to hold power after the 2022 midterms as Biden warned. Past midterm defeats, some monstrous, for the Democrats had amply proven that. The Democrats reversed that sad history with their success in the 2018 midterms. Now they were in a frantic race to make sure that their success in 2018 was not an aberration.

The clock was winding down fast in mid-2022 on that race.

·

5

The Disappearing Voter

"Speaker Nancy Pelosi and I had a productive meeting with the President during which he made one thing clear—he is all in on the midterms, and that starts with a significant investment in House races." New York congressman Sean Patrick Maloney, chairman of the Democratic Congressional Campaign, beamed when he told the press in February 2022 that Biden was "all in" on the 2022 midterms. He had just shown that, said Maloney, by gathering a group of key Democratic party leaders together at the White House.

At that meeting, Biden announced that he was immediately transferring 15 million dollars from the coffers of the Democratic National Committee to the House and Senate campaign committees. This was an unprecedented move by a president with the 2022 midterms still months away.

Biden made the move to add more muscle to the efforts of the campaign committees to get out the vote. The midterms were nine months off, and the clock was fast ticking down on the work the Democrats needed to do to keep as many Democrats as possible in office and hopefully put more Democrats in Congress.

There was little room for error. If just one Senate seat flipped to a GOP candidate, and seven or eight House seats flipped to GOP candidates, it could be the nightmare that then-President Obama experienced after the 2010 and 2014 midterms. The GOP completely took over the House and Senate in 2014. For the last two years of his second term, he was little more than a caretaker president. The GOP torpedoed all his major legislative initiatives, and many of his key judicial appointments, up to and including his SCOTUS pick Merrick Garland.

The fifteen million dollars that Biden authorized the transfer of from the DNC to the committees was the largest ever made at one time from the DNC to the two campaign committees. Campaign committee officials talked much about the sabotage of Obama's agenda during his last White House years. They were anxiously mindful that the same could happen to Biden if in the words of one, "Republicans take the Senate, they'll push the agenda of the ultra-wealthy and big corporations at the expense of working Americans."

The money Biden transferred was laser targeted to eight states. The traditional swing states where the question of which party would control one or both congressional chambers would be decided.

In part, Biden took the action he did releasing the money because the midterms were going to be a close run-up for the Democrats. And in part, because he and the DNC heard the loud complaints from many party officials and operatives that Biden and the DNC weren't doing enough to get Democrats out for the midterms.

Biden's move struck directly to the heart of more than just potential Democratic party laxity in priming voters to turn out. There was the implicit understanding that in the midterms a lot of people, particularly minorities, the young, and college-educated suburban women don't bother to vote. In the 2016 presidential election, nearly 137 million people voted. That was more than half of the vote-eligible population.

What really caught observers' eyes was that nearly one hundred million eligible persons didn't vote that year. The *U.S. Census Bureau* conducted a survey after the 2012 presidential election to find out why so many Americans didn't vote, and who they were. The answers non-voters gave were varied and curious. Many low-income voters said they stayed away from the polling place because of a disability or illness. Others cited "transportation problems," and still others chalked it up to "registration problems" or an "inconvenient polling place."

The figures were much better in 2020. Trump saw to that as the most controversial resident of the White House in decades. His celebrated taunts, digs, attacks, and over-the-top race and immigrant baiting stirred millions to mob the polls to either keep him in the White House or get him out of there. Seventeen million more people voted in 2020 than in 2016. That was sixty-seven percent of eligible adults. Overall, it was a five percent jump from 2016. Biden won in large part because moderate voters had enough of Trump and wanted him out.

Predictably, partisan voters cast their ballots along party lines. But many more moderate voters chose Biden over Trump in 2020, helping to propel the Democratic nominee to victory.

Here are the comparative voting figures for the 2016 versus the 2020 presidential election:

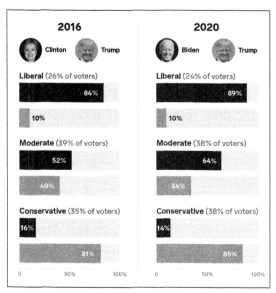

Source: Edison/Insider

In 2014, the GOP fully dominated House and Senate races, solidified control of Congress, and doomed Obama's second term. That year fully six in ten eligible adult voters stayed home. The bulk of them was young, Hispanic, and African American, less affluent, and less educated. The paltry midterm voter turnout stood in sharp contrast to the near-record number of African American voters that turned out for Obama's historic election in 2008. The numbers turnout was still high for his reelection bid in 2012.

The reason was simple. His candidacy was not seen as a candidacy, but as a crusade—a history-making crusade. Blacks did not just see this as a chance to put a Black president in office, but a chance to snatch a piece of history along the way.

Obama was seen not as a distant, remote, traditional presidential candidate, but almost as a family member—someone to embrace and take personal pride in their accomplishments. Many Blacks in the past were apathetic, lethargic, and indifferent to the political process because they thought their vote made no difference, or because of their antipathy to the Democrats, whom they accused of plantationism for taking the Black vote for granted and giving little in return.

Obama promised to reverse that once in the White House. It wasn't just Black voters though. His message of hope and change resonated and inspired the young, Hispanic, Asians, women, and LGBT voters to also make his election more than a normal election but a passion. Obama was not on the ballot in the 2010 or 2014 midterms. The hope and change message had long since either been satisfied, fulfilled for many, forgotten, or for some crashed in disappointment.

The operative word though was hope, hope for change, and a better future. Only then do voters feel a stake in the outcome, and that their vote can make a difference.

The *Pew Research Center* zeroed in on this issue of candidate likeability by crunching the numbers to determine why more people stayed home on Election Day in 2016 than in 2012. Many Hispanic registered voters who didn't vote said they didn't like the candidates or the campaign issues. Many white and Asian registered voters said the same thing. The turnout in 2016 was down across virtually all racial and ethnic voter demographics.

Among Black voters the numbers didn't just drop, they plunged. One in five Black nonvoters were candid when asked why they didn't vote. They said they didn't vote because they didn't like either Trump or Clinton or the issues they focused on. Or they simply were not interested. Again, this was in marked contrast to 2008 and 2012 with Obama on the ballot.

It's no accident that those least likely to vote in the midterms are young, minorities, and lower-income persons. They are traditionally the most marginalized, and the least apt to be the target of any prolonged, focused, civic, or political engagement effort by not just the GOP but Democrats too. It becomes a two-way street, the parties make no real effort to engage them, and in return, there's no real sense on their part of a need to engage in the political process. Policy issues are seen as remote, removed, or even non-existent in terms of having any direct connection or meaning to their lives.

The issue of poverty in America is a near-perfect example of this disconnect. Millions of Americans are below the federal poverty level. Millions of them are adult eligible voters. Yet, there is almost no mention of the word poverty let alone advocacy of specific programs to attack poverty on the campaign trail in presidential and midterm elections. There's a reason, in fact, several reasons, for this. One is trying to define who is poor.

One who doesn't have the problem of defining who is poor is a former long term welfare recipient. Cassandra (first name only preferred) knows poverty firsthand through many years of her and her children scraping by on food stamps and a never quite adequate welfare check. She now helps other welfare recipients in Cincinnati battle the tangle of bureaucratic loops many must go through to get payments. When asked why so many poor people don't vote, she minced no words, "Folks that are on welfare the politicians look down on us."

Apart from the visibly homeless, and those rummaging around on skid row, and in some of the poorest and most recognizable urban inner-city communities, one can easily be considered working, or even middle class, one day and the loss of a job, and tangible income, can quickly dump that person into the poverty ranks the next. This makes the poor even more diffuse, and hard to typecast. They cut across all ethnic, gender, religious, and even political party affiliation lines. There are also plenty of low-income persons in the South, Middle America, and the conservative rural areas, who vote GOP.

The other reason is that the poor do not have an advocacy group to go to bat for them with lawmakers such as labor, civil rights, education, environmental, or abortion rights supporters have. This further increases their political invisibility.

Presidential and congressional candidates fiercely arm wrestle over ways to best bring down the deficit, reduce spending, decrease taxes, and get rid of wasteful programs. They also spar hard over how best to protect the interests of the middle class. It's about votes, and a pro-middle-class, cut government spending line, appeals to centrists, and independents.

They, not the poor, are the voters the GOP and Democrats depend on to be the path to or back to the White House. The lack of engagement with the poor, disdain or at best indifference to them, coupled with the spate of laws that make it harder and harder for many persons to vote, all work in tandem to further ensure that millions tune out to politicians and politics.

The terrible reality is that parties are far more likely to woo, court, and aim their pitches at white middle-class voters in the crucial swing states. Minority, and especially minority low-income voters, and young voters are as the complaint is often heard taken for granted by the Democrats and routinely written off as not in play "for us" by the GOP.

* * * * *

The deliberate barriers that have been erected for poor and minority voters since 2010 to damp down their vote numbers are formidable. One is the availability and accessibility of polling places. There are fewer of them in minority communities. Surveys have found that in predominantly white suburban communities few persons say they have any problem finding a polling place. In African American and Hispanic neighborhoods, it's just the opposite. The lag in these communities is not haphazard or accidental.

Election officials make the call on where to put a polling place. They base their decision on factors such as population, accessibility, and location recognizability. They can eliminate a station, or move it, at their discretion. There's a Catch-22 here. Minorities vote in smaller numbers than whites. The smaller numbers mean fewer polling places in their neighborhoods.

The GOP-controlled state legislature in Texas, for instance, led the charge to close even more polling places in minority communities before the 2020 presidential election. The graph of the closures in one key county tells the sordid tale of suppression:

How Harris County's polling place distribution would change under SB 7.

All but two state House districts represented by Democrats in Harris County would see a reduction in Election Day polling places under the GOP's priority voting bill. In most cases, those districts have a far higher share of eligible voters of color than the districts that would gain voting sites.

How Harris County's polling place distribution would change under SB 7				
District	Party	Change in polling places	Registered voter population	White voting-age population
141	D	-11	84,010	10.6%
146	D	-8	93,243	23.6%
148	D	-8	93,517	41.6%
142	D	-7	95,301	18.1%
147	D	-7	117,099	29.7%
140	D	-6	66,250	12.0%
143	D	-6	71,313	17.6%
144	D	-6	63,477	26.0%
137	D	-5	57,295	28.2%
145	D	-4	76,258	22.1%
134	D	-3	143,792	70.5%
131	D	-1	91,910	11.7%
139	D	-1	102,879	17.8%
Note: White voting-age population is calculated from the U.S. Census Bureau's Citizen Voting Age by Race and Ethnicity (CVAP) numbers. Registered voter population is based on the 2020 general election.				

Source: Texas Legislative Council, Texas Secretary of State, and the U.S. Census Bureau

* * * * *

There's also the issue of language and the ballot. A ballot must be in the language of the relevant minority group. However, there are ways to skirt that. One way is crunching the numbers. The law states that the number of Limited English Proficiency (LEP) citizens of voting age must exceed 10,000 for the ballot to be in the language of the voters. That's 5 percent of all eligible voters. With all Native American reservation residents, the number must exceed 5 percent.

Another requirement is that the illiteracy rate of the minority population must also be higher than the national illiteracy rate. How and who determines what illiteracy is and who is illiterate? This is often little more than a judgment call. If the call is that there is no illiteracy issue or language issue in a particular voting district, that's heavily or exclusively minority, the legal requirement about language ballots goes out the window.

Some states make strenuous efforts to ensure that ballots are in native languages such as Chinese, Gujarati, Korean, and Spanish. They also must ensure there is no discrimination in polling placement, that same-day voting extends longer, and that there is wide use of mail-in balloting. The problem is these states are mostly lockdown Democratic voter states. California, for instance, has majority-minority voting numbers.

GOP governors and GOP-controlled state legislatures have moved in the opposite direction in their states to narrow down or outright scrap measures to ease voting. Yet, in states such as Florida, Georgia, and Texas, there are significant numbers of Black, Hispanic, and Native American voters there. Hispanic voters in particular make up a big, growing, and potentially potent political force in key Red States:

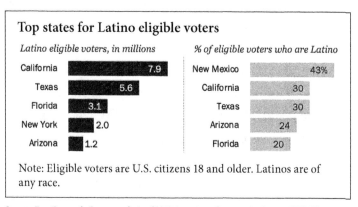

Source: Pew Research Center analysis of 2018 American Community Survey (PUMS).

Black, Hispanic, and lower-income persons have gotten much attention from political analysts, and pollsters, about non-voting. Yet, younger persons also have shown that when they do turn out in substantial numbers, they can also make a difference in the outcome of a race. They certainly proved that in 2008 when they were inspired by Obama's hope and change message. However, that was 2008. Young people far more than even older Blacks and Hispanics are likely to be absent from the polls, especially in the midterms.

Meanwhile, youth turnout nationally for midterms hovers around 20 percent. By comparison, the figure for turnout in the midterms for older adults is near 50 percent.

The reasons in many cases for the non-participation of younger voters are not much different than those cited for Blacks and Hispanics.

There are other factors at play in explaining their consistently low voter participation. One is the widespread complaint that many young people don't care much about the political process.

Kei Kawashima-Ginsberg, the director of CIRCLE " which is an initiative at Tufts University that studies youth civic and political participation notes, "Whenever young people are surveyed, there is a significant lack of knowledge about how exactly the government works, and, therefore, how their vote actually matters." In a survey she conducted shortly before the 2018 midterms of working-class youth, she found that nearly 20 percent of young persons professed ignorance of the ins and outs of politics and government. They just didn't know enough to be comfortable with voting.

The young, like many other non-voters, also took a jaundiced view of politics and politicians. They were convinced that their vote wouldn't do anything to change anything since the structure of politics seemed to be set in stone, Money, and power at the top, they insisted, ensured that the status quo remain firmly locked in place no matter who was in office.

In follow-up interviews with young people after the 2018 midterms, there was no change in their view. They still had a lower voter participation rate. They gave pretty much the same reasons why they didn't vote. They still didn't feel their vote mattered, they didn't care, they were too busy, or they didn't feel like they knew enough to vote.

* * * * *

Inevitably when the question is asked and debate arises over why so many Americans don't vote, a comparison is made to voter turnout in other democratic countries. The U.S. voting turnout numbers in comparison to the turnout for elections in other democratic countries certainly stir puzzlement and envy. In countries such as Belgium and Sweden, the voting numbers commonly nudge or top eighty percent. The U.S. ranks 26th out of thirty-two developed democracies in voting age election participation. A favorite game among political analysts is to nominate 'did not vote" as a candidate against both the Republican and Democratic presidential candidates. The "did not vote" candidate wins in a walkover every time.

Here's how much of a walkover:

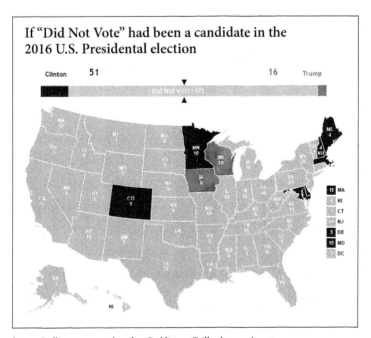

Source: Brilliantmaps.com based on Reddit user Taillesskangaru's posts.

The twenty-five countries with higher voter turnouts than the U.S. have one characteristic in common. They make it easier for their citizens to vote. Some countries skip the formal registration paperwork and bureaucracy. They automatically register all voting-age adults. Other countries let anyone who wants to vote online, and they automatically transfer their voter registration address if they move to wherever they move. Election Day registration and voting are also the norms in many countries. In the U.S., the states that encourage that have higher voter turnouts than those that don't.

While much is made of the voter suppression hurdles

put up by the GOP state legislatures, some countries go to the other extreme. They make voting mandatory. The absent voter in those countries is fined. There's also the time factor. In Western Europe, elections are not just one-day affairs. Voters are given extended time frames to vote, sometimes weeks before the election. These countries unlike the U.S. have potent third, fourth, and even multiple parties with solid constituencies. There are frequent run-offs. This further extends the period for voting. This stirs much more interest and excitement in voting.

* * * * *

The other way to answer the question of why so many Americans, particularly minorities, the poor, and the young, don't vote is to talk directly to them and ask why. One congressional district that fit the bill of a district with a lousy voting history, in fact, one of the lousiest in the country, was Arizona's Third Congressional District. The district is in a fought-over swing state and has a large number of minority and lower income-eligible adults of voting age.

More than two-thirds of the eligible voters in the district were Black or Hispanic, or Native American. Almost seventy percent of those vote eligible didn't vote. The adjoining Fifth Congressional District stood in stark contrast in voting. It had double the voter turnout in the 2016 presidential election than the Third District.

There was much hand wringing among Democrats in

2016 over the paltry voter turnout in that district. There was good reason for the angst. The likelihood was that in a heavily minority and low-income district, voters are almost certain to vote Democratic. However, that's a double-edged sword. The party is less likely to put the time, money, and energy, into an intense voter turnout effort with these voters. Their votes are viewed as virtually in the bag for the Democrats.

"There's an assumption made that these voters will just come," notes Third District congressional representative Raul Grijalva, "It's like … a cattle call." It's a vicious, self-reinforcing cycle. The Democratic party puts little effort into engagement, something as basic as at least having readily available voting materials in Spanish. Often even that isn't done. Therefore, there is no incentive for those eligible to vote to show up on Election Day

The voter turnout, though, dramatically bumps up when there is a concentrated effort made to get people to the polls. One Native American political group in the district provided rides to the polls and translated voting materials for new voters. In those precincts in the district, the percentage of voters sharply jumped in 2016 from what it was in 2012.

A jump in voting in certain elections and when real efforts are made to get people to the polls in certain districts are fine. However, they don't address the many varied reasons why so many Americans are vote resistant. The standard reasons are continually repeated in answer to why:

apathy, frustration, lack of information, social isolation, logistical barriers, economic volatility, technology use and complications in voting, and of course the vote suppression ploys.

They are all valid reasons. One other significant factor in determining whether someone will make the effort to go to the polls is the candidates themselves. Countless polls and surveys through nearly every election cycle, be it presidential or the midterms, have continually found that there is no "ideal" candidate that non-voters or even voters can say whom they feel addresses all or most of their views and concerns. The disillusionment with the candidates is deep-seated in American politics. There's the feeling that politicians lie, cheat, cut corners, make inflated promises, and simply say what they think whichever group of voters they are talking to want to hear.

There is much disgust among many Americans that candidates and incumbents engage in the politics of negativism. That is tossing as much mud on each other as they can at the expense of engaging voters and providing them with intelligible information on the compelling issues. This deepens the belief that politics is a dirty business in which big-money special interests, corporations and the wealthy call the shots.

But how negative is negative, and how does it turn potential voters into non-voters? A team of Illinois Wesleyan University researchers wanted answers to those questions. They examined state exit poll data for presidential, senatorial, and gubernatorial elections from 2000-to 2010. They concluded that negative advertising and negative political attacks did turn off many would-be voters.

They also found that in some campaigns negative attacks and advertising did energize some voters. The problem for the Democrats, though, is that the voters motivated to flock to the polls because of negative attacks were more likely to vote Republican, and the negative ads and attacks were by Republican candidates. The study then took it right back to the main point that those not already aligned with the GOP reacted with disgust to negative campaigning, and were more likely to stay home on Election Day.

*****

There is yet one more reason why tens of thousands of vote age-eligible adults in the U.S. don't vote. They can't. A staggering one in 13 Blacks is nearly permanently frozen out from the voting booth. They are ex-felons. During the 2004 presidential campaign then-Democratic presidential candidate John Kerry mildly protested the towering hurdles to ex-felon voting in dozens of states. Kerry raised the issue for a good reason. He was trying to unseat Republican incumbent President George Bush Jr. He remembered what happened with the last Democratic candidate, Al Gore, in the 2000 presidential contest.

Gore disputedly and arguably lost Florida to Bush by a few hundred votes. That cost him the White House.

Those few hundred votes almost certainly could have been easily swamped by thousands of Democratic voters in the state. A substantial portion of those Democratic votes would have come from Black voters. But thousands of those Black voters weren't there because they were permanently banned from the polls. They were among the thousands of ex-felons that Florida bars from the polls for life. It makes no difference if the ex-felon is imprisoned for petty drug use or murder. If it's a felony conviction they're out.

A handful can and do appeal to Florida's Governor and do win their appeal to have the permanent ban lifted. However, the loops they must go through are tortuous, arbitrary, and humiliating. Florida was back in the news in 2018 with a voter initiative, the Voter Restoration Amendment. It would lift the ex-felon voting lifetime ban.

The ban had nothing to do with protecting society, preserving order, or punishment. It had everything to do with politics and race. They can't be separated. It was no accident that the states that imposed the medieval lifetime or close to lifetime bans on ex-felons, like Florida, are mostly Deep South states.

The bans were a naked, blatant, 21st Century update of the old Jim Crow disenfranchisement ploys the South used for decades to dilute the Black vote. The arsenal of racially abusive tactics included poll taxes, literacy laws, and political gerrymandering to drive Blacks from the voting booths. The states are all GOP-controlled. The resistance from the GOP governors and state legislatures to modifying, let alone scrapping the harsh felon bans, has been fierce.

This thinly disguised relic of the South's Jim Crow past has done much to drastically dilute Black political strength. In the 2016 presidential election, if the one million Black men in prison, on parole, or on probation that were disenfranchised because of their criminal record had been added to the total their vote might have made a crucial difference in deciding the White House as well as close statewide contests in the midterms too.

Black ex-felon disenfranchisement will probably get worse. Blacks still make up nearly half of the more than two million prisoners in the nation's jails. The continued entrenchment of racially biased drug laws, racial profiling, and chronic poverty in many Black communities means that more Black men will be arrested, prosecuted, convicted, and serve longer prison sentences than white men. This virtually guarantees that the number of Blacks behind bars will swell. This means continued fewer potential voters, mostly for the Democrats.

The Sentencing Project estimates that at the rate of Black incarceration since 2016 upwards of 40 percent of Black men could be permanently barred from the polls in the vote-restricted states in the 2022 midterms and the 2024 presidential election. Many conservatives passionately defend the policy of ex-felon disenfranchisement. They claim that barring criminals from voting society sends the strong message that if you break the law, you should pay and continue to pay dearly.

The argument might make sense if all or most of the disenfranchised ex-felons were convicted murderers, rapists, or robbers. And they were denied the vote because of a court-imposed sentence. This is not the case. None of the states that bar felons from voting in near perpetuity require that judges strip them of their voting rights as part of their sentence based on the seriousness of the crime or the severity of the punishment.

Most ex-felons are jailed for non-violent crimes such as drug possession, passing bad checks, or auto theft. In most instances, they fully served their sentence and in theory, paid their debt to society. Most of the convicted felons were young men when they committed their crimes. The odds are that most of them wouldn't become career criminals, but would hold steady jobs, raise families, and become responsible members of the community.

Yet imprinting these ex-felons with the legal and social stigma of "hereditary criminals" and banning them from voting until death makes politicians and many Americans seem like the worst kind of hypocrites when they say they believe in giving prisoners a second chance in life.

Biden tersely addressed the issue in a presidential campaign talking point in April 2019, "We need to make sure formerly incarcerated individuals who have served their sentences are able to fully participate in our democracy." It wasn't much. The Democrats have suffered the most from the bans, as they were intended by the mostly GOP controlled legislatures and governors that have kept them in place. Yet, he made no call for any federal initiative to prod the states to toss or at least modify the felon voting bans.

That task has been left mostly to civil liberties groups and civil rights organizations to fight hard against the bans. They have filed court challenges and mounted a sustained lobbying campaign in Congress or state legislatures to get the discriminatory voting laws changed. The denial of voting rights to thousands of Blacks, decades after the end of slavery and legal segregation is a travesty of justice and a blot on the democratic process.

The blot has a special significance in the midterms. Even in the best of times, voter turnout will always be lower in the midterms than in presidential elections. Eliminating one in thirteen Blacks near permanently from the polls in elections with a lower voter turnout, and where every vote could have enormous significance in some key swing states has an even greater impact than in the general election. Those votes can make the difference between a win or a loss for a candidate in a tight race, especially if that candidate or incumbent is a Democrat.

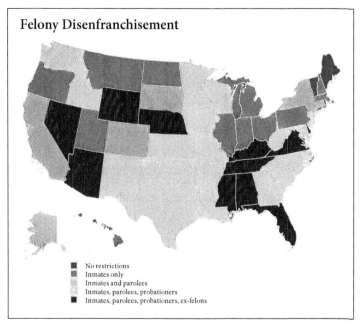

Source: Sentencing Project

* * * * *

There is an ominous flip side to the issue of why so many Americans don't vote. That's why so many who do vote particularly in the midterms vote against their interests. They are largely lower-income, less educated, politically marginalized, and generally ignored in the political outreach efforts of Democrats and the GOP. The prime difference is that many of them are white.

For decades GOP presidents and legislators backed deep cuts in programs that would slash Medicare and supported partial privatizing of Social Security. They would turn Medicaid, food stamps, housing vouchers, welfare, and other federal programs entirely over to the states. The moment that ever happened, many cash-strapped states would reduce, if not wholesale eliminate benefits, and impose an even more incredible tangle of choking eligibility regulations on potential recipients.

If states ever got federal block grants to administer Medicaid, the likelihood of cuts was great. States, for instance, such as Mississippi, when faced with funding shortfalls, could cap enrollment, cut eligibility, stop offering mandatory benefits, and lower provider reimbursements to the needy.

An assessment of the impact of states handling the federal funding of Medicaid was not pretty. For instance, in Red State Alaska, GOP officials considered applying for block grant funding for Medicaid in 2015. $270 million would be cut in state Medicaid funding and $480 million reduced in federal expenditures. The result: the loss of thousands of jobs in the health service industries, an almost certain tax increase, and a sharp reduction in Medicaid coverage.

Yet, GOP officeholders and candidates in national and state elections since the late 1960s have netted most of the white votes in the Deep South and Heartland states. Whichever candidate gets the GOP presidential nomination will get most of the white votes in the general and midterm elections in those states. White voters in the poorest of Deep South states have been money in the vote bank for GOP presidential candidates Nixon, Reagan, Bush Sr. George W. Bush, and especially Trump.

These voters have also been political money in the bank for GOP candidates and incumbents in the midterms. These voters make possible the GOP's massive electoral wins and domination of state legislatures in those states.

The theories to explain why so many blue-collar and poor whites repeatedly and reliably vote against themselves abound. The contention is that their votes are protests against the perceived decay of traditional religious and moral values and a push back against what they perceive as a dangerous socialist drift of the country. They are thumbing their noses at the liberal elites, intellectuals, automaton bureaucrats, and the social engineers in Washington.

One man and his small Minnesota town were profiled by the *New York Times* in the months before the 2012 presidential election. He was by any definition lower income. He worked a series of part-time jobs to make ends meet. The town suffered from a loss of key industries. So, he was by no means alone living with his marginal economic plight, even desperation.

He like many others in the town was forced to rely on government programs for assistance such as the Earned Income Tax Credit, free school breakfasts for his children, and Medicare. These were all Democratic Party stamped programs. Yet that did not make him think any kinder of government or Democrats. If anything, his attitude was one of resentment, "I don't demand that the government does this for me," he said. "I don't feel like I need the government."

There's some truth to these contentions. Tea Party

leaders and followers during the Obama White House years masterfully mined those sentiments while piling on a healthy dose of bombast at the federal government for alleged reckless spending, extravagant social programs, and clawing away at personal freedoms and liberties. They posed themselves as the champions of the average person and woman. This fakery worked masterfully for the GOP and did much to aid the party's triumph in the 2010 and 2014 midterms.

Railing at the elites and out-of-touch bureaucrats that allegedly run government would not in itself have whipped thousands into hysteria against Obama and the Democrats. The cry of runaway spending, profligate social programs, and assaults on liberty masked the rage of many poor and working-class whites at a government they fervently believed was in the business of giving the company store away to the minority poor.

To many, government spending and programs are tantamount to handouts to undeserving Blacks and the poor, which in turn equals money snatched from the pockets of hard-working whites. Citing statistics and figures, and charts to show that more whites benefit from and depend on these entitlement programs than Blacks and Latinos was unlikely to sway those who believe government serves the minority poor away from voting for GOP candidates who will snatch these benefits away—pure, raw, unvarnished emotionalism grounded in deep-seated stereotypes, and bigotry that always trumped logic.

These are the voters who do show up at the polls, particularly during the midterms, and often play a leading role in hotly contested congressional races between Democrats and Republicans. Yet when it comes to voting for candidates that are most likely to champion their interests from affordable health care to living wage jobs, they don't support them. This is the perverse side of engaging in the political process while non-engaging on the issues that are vital to their well-being.

Biden's unprecedented act of publicly plowing $15 million in the Democratic House and Senate campaign committee's rally the troops' effort for the 2022 midterms was not an act of desperation. It was an acknowledgment that in the midterms far more than presidential elections a lot fewer voters show up on Election Day.

Biden was spending the extra money on the off chance that it would nudge up the number of Democratic voters even a couple of percentage points in the handful of nail-biter races that could determine control of the House or Senate or both in 2022. If the money could tip the scales for the Democratic candidate and get more traditional Democratic-leaning non-voters to the midterm polls, then the money had to be spent.

The GOP House and Senate campaign committees for their part made clear they were going for broke in spending on the 2022 midterms.

The GOP and the Democrats firmly laid the gauntlet down.

6

Breaking the Democrats' Midterm Jinx

McConnell was back in his home state of Kentucky in early November 2021. He was speaking to local groups about events in Washington. When he was asked about the 2022 midterms he especially perked up.

"And I think the key to '22 is to have a discussion with the American people about how they feel about the new administration and the Democratic Congress and what they're doing. So, I think the election will be about the future, not about the past." Then he had a prediction, "the midterms are likely to be a very good election for Republicans."

McConnell's glowing take on the midterms then a year away echoed what a parade of other pundits and political analysts were saying—Biden, and the Democrats were in big political trouble. It was repeated so often in blaring headlines that one got the feeling the midterm elections were over. Voting was just a formality. Biden even took the unusual step in April 2022, less than five months before the November midterms, to announce that some key White House staff members would be leaving.

Biden did not say that their departure was related to a possible midterm Democratic loss. However, the inference was that the midterm results could have an enormous influence on White House staffing for the remaining two years of his term. In the wake of that, the refrain continued that Democrats and Biden would get hammered and would lose the House or the Senate or both.

That the president's party was likely to come out on the short end of the political stick in midterms was backed up by countless midterm election result studies. They repeatedly showed that the president's party more often than not suffered midterm losses, sometimes colossal losses, in both the House and Senate. The losses have often been enough to flip one or both congressional chambers, as well as many state races.

That happened in 1946 when the GOP took back the House and the Senate. It happened again in 1958. This time the Democrats took back both the House and the Senate. It happened again in 1974, 1994, 2006, 2010, and 2014. The reversal of political fortunes for either the Democrats or Republicans in the midterms has done much to ensure that the president's party will suffer reverses is ground in stone whenever there's speculation about the outcome of a pending midterm election.

However, it is not inevitable that the president's party will lose every midterm election. It certainly wasn't foreordained that Biden and the Democrats would suffer a tsunami wave in lost seats and even control of the House or Senate or both in the 2022 midterms. Many of the midterm elections have seen minimal or modest losses or gains for the two parties. Biden could take consolation that any Democratic losses in some past midterm contests were offset by Democratic wins in other contests.

At the same time, though, the incontestable fact was that the GOP had a game plan in 2022 for taking back Congress which it openly espoused. The plan centered on reviving the cultural wars it used to devastating effect in the 1980s and 1990s. The contentious issues then were abortion, gay rights, and affirmative action. In 2022, the current issues were an alleged crime surge, critical race theory, and transgenderism.

Take Critical Race Theory. Here's what an Economist/You Gov Poll in June 2021 found:

- 86 percent of Democrats expressing a favorable view of the theory
- 94 percent of Republicans expressed an unfavorable view
- 76 percent of Independents expressed an unfavorable
- 55 percent of respondents overall said it was bad for America
- 75 percent of African Americans said it was good for the country

The GOP aimed to exploit the political fault lines, polarize and inflame its core voters, the less educated, white rural, blue-collar, and evangelicals prodding them to storm the polls in anger and revolt on midterm Election Day. The January 6, 2021, Capitol insurrection gave a bitter and ominous preview of the potential for revving up legions of Trump and rightist voters to swing into political action.

To the GOP's horror, this also posed a potentially damaging problem for the party in the 2022 midterms. Several GOP candidates for congressional offices either participated in the takeover rally or refused to back away from support of the rally's stated bellicose aims. Democratic party leaders were unabashed in waving the January 6 insurrection before voters; reminding them that more than a few House Republicans backed the lawless rally that preceded the takeover, and that lots of GOP House members refused to condemn Trump for inciting the mob.

In May 2021, GOP House lawmakers had a second chance to show their disdain of the Trump incited Capitol riot. House Democrats had gotten what they thought was GOP agreement to fully back the establishment of a select committee to investigate the causes of the pandemonium of January 6. The deal quickly unraveled when masses of Trump and GOP backers voiced outrage at the committee idea. House Minority Leader Kevin McCarthy who initially agreed to name GOP members to the committee, reneged on the agreement.

He didn't stop there. He publicly thundered that House

GOP members would totally boycott the committee. Meanwhile in the Senate, McConnell and GOP senators didn't even bother going through the motions and discussing conducting a January 6 riot investigation. There would be none.

This more than suited one man to a tee. In a tweet at the start of the committee hearings, an unbowed Trump ridiculed what he branded "the unselect committee" and railed that "January 6th was not simply a protest, it represented the greatest movement in the history of our Country to Make America Great Again. It was about an Election that was Rigged and Stolen, and a Country that was about to go to HELL..& look at our Country."

Minnesota GOP House representative Tom Emmer almost certainly didn't dispute that sentiment. He not only attended the rally but also headed the National Republican Congressional Committee which was tasked with getting more GOP House representatives elected in the midterms. He expressed no remorse for participating in the insurrectionary mobbing nor condemned anyone who did. Worse still, he seemed to advocate getting more insurrectionists that stormed Congress elected, "The beauty of this country is that anybody who wants to run for office can. I want as many people as possible who share our values to step up and be the voice and run for office."

The good news for Democrats was that a poll the Democratic Congressional Campaign Committee conducted in July 2021 found that this kind of head in the sand backdoor cheerleading of lawlessness by a top gun in the GOP midterm campaign machine turned off a lot of voters in the must-win battleground states. The poll claimed that voters in these states told pollsters that they had serious doubts about GOP lawmakers after hearing that those members "helped spread Trump's lie about the election."

Many Democrats also hoped that the GOP might aid and abet the Democrats in the 2022 midterms by putting up another motley pack of borderline political kooks, cranks, and misfits. This would make independents and even some Republicans gag in disgust and stay home or vote for a Democrat.

That happened in the 2010 midterms when they lost two Senate seats in Delaware and Nevada, they seemed almost shoo-ins to win. In each state, the GOP brushed aside established party regulars with solid political and vote gathering credentials. Instead, the party-backed two Tea Party far out, borderline eccentric, stalwarts for the Senate races.

The GOP did it again in a special Alabama Senate election in 2017. It backed Judge Roy Moore, whose wacko comments, lascivious conduct, and thinly disguised racist rants, assured that a Democrat would do the politically impossible and win a general election race in the deep-Red State of Alabama.

* * * * *

It was always possible that the GOP might slip again and do the same in some 2022 midterm races. However, it was risky business to depend on the political enemy to beat themselves. The Trump win in 2016 was the ultimate proof of that.

Two proven factors that determine how well the president's party may perform in the midterms is how effective his party is in getting the biggest turnout possible of its supporters and potential supporters. The determinant to that is a well-structured, finely targeted outreach effort and effective messaging of the president and the party's legislative achievements. The party must convince voters that those achievements directly benefit them.

The other factor is to hope that memories of things that unraveled during the president's first two years are short. And conversely, voters retain good memories of things that went right especially concerning the all-important economy and the issue of security.

Much of the responsibility for putting that game plan into action rests at the top with the respective national party committees. The RNC and the DNC. With Biden and the Democrats in the White House and with the most to lose from a GOP midterm edge out, the ball for the 2022 midterm was squarely in the DNC's court. There was good and bad history for the DNC to draw on in the quest to get the maximum number of bodies to the polls and punch the Democratic ticket.

A starting point for examining the task of the respective party campaign committees is the 2016 presidential campaign. The Democratic National Committee was by any standard a wreck and a ruin during the 2016 presidential campaign. It got pounded for misstep after misstep, which included: poor, and disconnected leadership, leaked emails, gross favoritism, petty infighting, blatant manipulation of the primaries, and gross cluelessness about the Trump threat.

In the aftermath of the Trump election debacle, there was fierce jockeying for the top spot to head the DNC. The main issue was that the Democrats had to convince many potential younger, more progressive voters that it was not a handmaiden centrist, compromising, top-heavy corporate-backed, and run party. If it couldn't shake that image, it could kiss millions of progressive voters goodbye. The party's voter turnout efforts with that segment of voters would have about as much energy as a burned-out battery in trying to fire up voters for the crucial 2018 mid-terms.

The counter was that the Democrats flopped precisely because Trump bagged an enormous chunk of the angry, alienated, and frustrated blue-collar and rural whites. The Democrats could try and get many of them back by crafting an appealing message to them about runaway jobs and economic security. This supposedly required a Democrat in the mold of Obama to do it. There were two truths behind the clashing views of what a DNC chair and the committee should be and where they should take the party. Both would be sorely tested in the 2018 midterms and again in the 2022 midterms.

The Democratic National Committee is tasked with the chore of spotting and recruiting able talent to run as

Democrats for office. Then it must help to raise money for the Democratic candidates and incumbents, put volunteer and paid professional boots on the ground for their campaigns, and mount an all-out get out the vote blitz in the weeks leading up to both the midterms and presidential elections to put Democrats locally and nationally over the top.

Again, this takes a smooth functioning, well-coordinated ground game to put as many Democrats as possible in Congress and to keep the ones who are there in office. That's only the start. It also takes someone who can inspire, cajole, and engage legions of Hispanics, Blacks, and youth voters who were absent from the polls in 2016. Though Biden won the presidency in 2020, many of them still did not vote in that election. An even greater number of them have been chronic no-shows in prior midterm elections.

The other disturbing truth was that Trump won many disconnected and frustrated white voters to his banner. He welded their latent racist, anti-immigrant, anti-woman, pseudo-patriotic sentiment to their loathing of, and alienation from, the GOP establishment and the Democrat's beltway, out of touch with the Main Street crowd. That was a tough hurdle for a progressive or a centrist Democrat to overcome. The better option for the DNC remained to pad the number of Hispanics, Blacks, women, and youth in the five or six states that elect presidents.

The gaping disparity between the GOP and Democrats in voter turnout in the 2016 primaries was not in the tens of thousands but millions. The GOP energized its base like it hadn't done in years, as well as firing up lots of young persons who in years past would likely not have been caught dead voting for a GOP presidential candidate. At the same time, the Democratic turnout was to be charitable, tepid in comparison to the vote totals Obama racked up in winning the swing states in 2008 and 2012. This fall-off came in the face of the spirited, impassioned face-off between Hillary Clinton and Bernie Sanders. His populist hit Wall Street hard message touched a huge nerve among legions of young and not so young voters.

Clinton did decisively beat Trump in the popular vote. But her leading vote margin came from the more populous Democratic front-loaded states in the East and West Coasts.

* * * * *

The universal consensus is that future elections will come down to which party can get the greatest number of voters to the polls to vote for their candidate in every race from the White House to congressional and statewide offices. In the 2014 midterms, and in the states Trump needed to win in 2016, the GOP showed that it could get those numbers out. Despite the GOP's well-tuned ground game and Trump's phony man-of-the-people, anti-Washington establishment hucksterism in 2016 and again in 2020, the Democrats still had a voter edge of several million over the GOP at the close of the 2020 presidential race. This was huge for the DNC leadership.

Its counterpart on the other side of the political coin, the Republican National Committee, also crunched the vote numbers and knew the Democrats had the inherent advantage in real and potential voters. In the early months of 2022, the RNC did not outraise the Democrats by massive amounts in donations. So, there was no real edge there either. Instead, the RNC took another tact to eliminate the voter disparity gap with the Democrats.

It announced in February 2022 that it would put a gigantic number of paid staffers and volunteers on the ground in a dozen or more targeted states. The GOP would arm its workers with the best and most sophisticated data on likely GOP voters, where to find them, and how to tailor their message to them. The RNC planned much more. It would spread the data wealth around making sure that thousands of state and local party committees had the voter data at hand and were trained in how to effectively use the data.

The task remained not just getting GOP loyalists to the polls. But also converting, in GOP strategist's parlance, "flipping" voters. That presumably meant independents and conservative Democrats. RNC officials repeatedly talked about having face-to-face conversations with potential supporters in the targeted states. This was not just paper talk.

The RNC had battle-tested the targeting campaign in special elections in 2021 in Virginia where it managed to bag the top state offices. In New Jersey, it won a number of seats in the state legislature. This was no small feat in a state considered a solidly blue state.

It was also no small feat to increase the number of African American voters that the GOP typically gets. That number is usually single digit. However, a small bump up in the number of Black and Hispanic voters for a GOP candidate in a tight race could make a difference. So, the RNC, as it did in past midterm and presidential elections, allocated a small amount of funding to what passed as its version of a Black outreach program. It coupled that with a high visibility media and promotional campaign for the handful of Black GOP candidates that it put up in a few key state and congressional races in midterm elections.

The RNC also took a page from Biden and the DNC's money playbook. It shelled out even more millions in early 2022 to state Senate and House campaign committees. These were deemed "critical investments" to ensure close coordination and direction of the efforts of the RNC to boost voter turnout.

The DNC and RNC though operating from polar opposites of the political spectrum had one thing in common in the run-up to the 2022 midterms. They viewed the midterms as important, if not more important, in some ways than the presidential election. No matter who sat in the White House, if Congress, preferably both wings, were not controlled by the president's party, it would virtually render him almost a lame duck for the remainder of his term. It would shackle and obstruct his legislative agenda. The midterms had almost replaced the presidential elections as the name of the game in national and state politics.

The predictions of doom for the Democrats in the 2022 midterms were based on the somewhat exaggerated history of how the president's party did in prior midterm elections: namely poorly. However, they were just predictions until the votes were actually in and counted. Biden, and the Democratic National Committee, though, did have a challenging task ahead of them to make sure the predictions weren't borne out.

* * * * *

Elections come down to which party can get the greatest number of voters to the polls to vote for their candidate for any and every congressional and statewide office. The Democrats showed that in the 2018 midterms they could get the numbers out. The trick was to build on the successes of the Obama, Sanders, and Biden presidential campaigns as well. They virtually single-handedly revved up a huge part of the Democratic base that was anemic, lukewarm, and even hostile to many Democratic candidates.

Obama forged his winning coalition based less on political interest than on his charisma and the passion for him. He stirred the feeling that his election was a big break from the stodgy, backroom, good ole boys, big money controlled, politics of Washington bureaucrats and hacks. Therefore, many disconnected voters came out in messianic droves in the 2008 and 2012 elections and tipped several of the crucial swing states to him. Without their numbers, those elections might easily have been real cliffhangers, if not a Democratic defeat, especially in 2012.

Unfortunately, the momentum wasn't sustained in the 2010 and 2014 midterms. Obama and the Democrats suffered near historic losses and lost control of Congress. It wasn't just hostility toward Obama with a strong whiff of racial bias on the part of many white conservative voters. The Democrats failed utterly to translate his popularity with the freshly minted voters who voted for the first time in the 2008 and 2012 presidential elections for Obama into renewed enthusiasm for the midterms.

Obama's success was a double-edged sword. The Democrats took too much for granted about his ability to continue to pull voters out in off-year elections without significant new voter organizing and mobilizing work on their part.

The 2022 midterms offered yet another special challenge and cause for concern among Democrats. Pollsters were having a field day beginning almost the moment Biden won the White House in trying to track which party's voters were the most enthusiastic about the midterms. For the most part, the polls showed anywhere from a slight to a modest GOP voter enthusiasm edge over the Democrats. What was more disconcerting was that even that might not have told the whole story about the likely voters in 2022?

There was great suspicion that the polls were getting it wrong about GOP enthusiasm. They were polling registered voters. However, there was no guarantee that just because they were registered, they would vote in the midterms. This could skew the numbers since there were far more registered Democrats than registered Republicans nationally.

The issue of who would vote then came back to not mere registration, but actual enthusiasm to vote. This has proven to be a far more reliable bellwether of how a party would fare in the election than just the registration numbers.

In the months before the 2018 midterms, polls showed a far greater level of enthusiasm among Democrats than Republicans. The numbers were staggering. Almost one hundred percent of those who said they were "extremely enthusiastic" about the election were adamant that they were going to vote. It's safe to say that one hundred percent of them didn't vote. However, it's equally safe to say that a big percentage of them kept their word and voted.

The edge here in 2018 went to the Democrats. It translated into the recapture of the House. Conversely, GOP voters told pollsters they were more "enthusiastic" about the 2010 and 2014 midterms. They were as good as their word then too. The GOP captured the House and the Senate.

The polls continued to show a close correlation between voter enthusiasm for the midterms and whether there was a Republican or Democratic in the White House. In every midterm election since the late 1970s, more voters from the opposing party had greater enthusiasm for the midterms. The average was three to five percentage points higher. This was not an insignificant number. In a close congressional race in a swing state, the percentage uptick could and often did prove the winning margin for a Republican or Democratic candidate.

It was a much different story if one party held a double-digit bulge over the opposition party in enthusiasm. It was a sure bet that that party would score big in the midterms.

How big? Here are the numbers.

- 2006: D+13 in high interest (Democrats picked up 30 House seats)
- 2010: R+17 (GOP picked up 63 House seats)
- 2014: R+11 (GOP picked up 13 House seats)
- 2018: D+9 (Democrats picked up 40 House seats)

* * * * *

Obama who was on the wrong end of the Democrat's disastrous midterm losses in the 2010 and 2014 midterms certainly understood the importance of arduous work and correct messaging as a signpost to midterm gains. In April 2022, he was back at the White House for a special celebration of the passage of his signature Affordable Care Act. At a press conference, before he departed the White House, he declared that the Democrats "got a story to tell" but just need "to tell it. " It was part urging, part warning, and all truth in what the Democrats had to do to avoid the predicted GOP surge that could cost them the House and Senate in the 2022 midterms.

He didn't say it directly, but the implication was that Biden's diminished poll ratings, high inflation, high gas prices, and jitters over Russia's attack on Ukraine were cause for real worry by the Democrats. A week before his White House visit and warning about the midterms, an NBC News poll released in March 2022, showed that there was a 17-point gap in enthusiasm between Republicans and Democrats heading into the election as well.

%9-10 Interest in the election by key subgroups			
Ranked by net difference	October 2021	January 2022	Net difference (Oct. 2021-Jan. 2022)
All Voters			
All	59%	51%	-8%
Blacks	60%	39%	-21%
Democratic primary Biden voters	70%	53%	-17%
West coast voters	61%	46%	-15%
Urban core county voters	62%	48%	-14%
Moderate voters	62%	48%	-14%
High school or less	58%	46%	-12%
Core Democratic Subgroups			
All	59%	51%	-8%
Democrats of color	63%	42%	-21%
Blacks	60%	39%	-21%
Male Democrats	62%	43%	-19%
Democrats ages 18-49	48%	31%	-17%
Democratic primary Biden voters	70%	53%	-17%
Urban core/ring county Democrats	62%	46%	-16%
Democrats < college	55%	40%	-15%
Urban core county voters	62%	48%	-14%

Source: POS, NBC News

Biden also spoke at the press conference. He implored Democrats to run on and take ownership of the mostly positive record of achievements in his first two years in the White House.

"We have a record—a record to be proud of; an agenda that addresses the biggest concerns here in America, in people's lives; the message that resonates. Now what we have to do is we have to sell it with confidence, clarity, conviction, and repetition."

If anything, Biden was the ultimate political realist. He drew the right lessons from the Democrats' capture of the House in the 2018 midterms. The first lesson was that the 2018 midterms were by no means a voter referendum coronating the Democrats as the party that the majority of Americans preferred. True, the Democrats did message correctly in some important races, spent money adroitly on candidates and incumbents that had a realistic chance to win or be reelected, and did put lots of troops on the ground in crucial districts. However, the 2018 midterms were a referendum not on the party but on Trump. The GOP's snatch back in the 2020 presidential election of many congressional seats it lost in the 2018 midterms was a sobering reminder of that.

Exit polls showed that over one-third of voters went to the polls out of anger at and loathing of Trump. They wanted to send a message that he and his administration represented everything odious to them. Since he was not on the ballot, the only way to do that was to vote for a congressional or state office Democrat. Ninety percent voted for the Democratic House candidate. While 88 percent of those who approved of Trump voted for the Republican House candidate.

Meanwhile, a whopping two-thirds of the voters were even more pointed about the Senate. If they were hostile to Trump, they backed the Democratic candidate or incumbent. If they liked Trump, they backed the GOP candidate or incumbent. In either case, Trump's imprint loomed large on the midterms.

By then Trump's overall approval rating was nestled in the low forties. It never moved much beyond that during his first two years in the White House. The vote was a total reversal from the 2014 midterms when more Republicans went to the polls than Democrats. The Trump effect also spurred more centrist independents to rush to the polls in 2018 than in 2014. The majority voted for a Democrat. Even more heartening, there were a lot of new voters in 2018. Almost twenty percent of the midterms' voters said they voted for the first time.

How Democrats won the House		
	Democrat	Republican
Voters under 30	67%	31%
Black voters	90%	9%
Hispanic voters	68%	30%
Women	59%	39%

Margin of error ± 3 pts.
Source: CBS News Poll

Biden learned one more lesson from the 2018 midterms. He, not Trump, was in the White House. There was no emotional incentive in the 2022 midterms for Democrats, let alone potentially new voters, to storm the polls for him. If anything, the GOP had the emotional edge, and drive to make the midterms a referendum on the president and his party. This as mentioned was borne out by the early polls in 2022 that showed a much higher level of enthusiasm among the GOP rank and file for the 2022 midterms than Democrats.

There was one more lesson Biden learned. Many voters were extremely issue conscious. In 2018, the issue was health care. A lot of voters had benefited from Obamacare. Trump and the GOP continued to wage a non-stop, hardball war against it. They filed mountains of lawsuits, and court challenges, passing limiting bills in GOP-controlled state legislatures. The disgust and fear among many Americans that the GOP might get its way and dump or roll back health care gains were palpable. A clear majority of voters backed Democratic candidates out of fear of health care rollbacks.

In 2022, health care had receded to the backburner of voter concern. The SCOTUS and various courts had firmly ensconced the ACA as law. Health care concern in 2018 was replaced by soaring inflation and soaring gas price concerns in 2022. Both were issues that Biden rightly or wrongly was identified with.

* * * * *

Once again, the always crucial indicator of the public mood on the direction they believed the country was going was the economy. It had little to do with how low the unemployment rate was or even how secure they actually were financially. It came down to a personal perception of how well the individual believed that they and their family were doing. In 2022, Biden as he correctly reminded voters had strong numbers on job creation and the low joblessness.

However, that didn't alter the belief among millions of Americans that even if they were employed and had a decent income, that things could fall apart for them at any moment. The paper numbers on high employment meant nothing. It was their sense of well-being that meant everything to them. The perception that things would get better or worse for them fastened squarely on the most visible target for praise or blame for that perception. That was the President.

One figure though was revealing about the perception of the public that things would get better or worse in the future. Less than ten percent of respondents in one poll in December 2021 said their income was going up faster than the cost of living. This was a shaky view of the future.

There was one final lesson Biden learned about how to combat public doubts and negativism of voters before elections. That was for Democrats to hammer away on their successes in fighting the pandemic, getting a massive job, and spending relief and infrastructure bill through Congress. Then continually seek ways to improve and expand health care delivery in the country. He urged that Democrats hit the GOP hard on their renewed assault on abortion and making cost-effective prescription drugs available.

These were two issues that might resonate with a majority of Americans, especially in the must-win swing states and among independents. Democrats had to avoid taking the GOP's bait and getting into a shouting match over such things as crime and critical race theory.

The crime issue, though, might be tough though to skirt since well into 2022, crime still ranked at or near the top as a major concern for voters. So much so that voters in two of the nation's most liberal, and top-heavy Democratic run cities, San Francisco and Los Angeles sent a message about crime in primary elections in June 2022.

In San Francisco, they recalled a liberal reform District Attorney who they charged was too soft on punishment. In Los Angeles voters, propelled a former conservative Republican turned Democrat mayoral candidate to the front of the pack in a primary election race for mayor.

Still. crime and critical race theory were cultural war issues that were emotional and potentially diversionary. Biden's counter was that he and no other swing state Democrat supported defunding the police. As for critical race theory, it was a non-issue in nearly every school district in the country.

Biden and the Democrats were right to be worried that

the 2022 midterms could be an awfully close run-up. There was the history of the president's party suffering losses. There was a GOP that would pull out all stops to win and take back control of Congress. Finally, there were the president's lowered approval ratings.

The task for the Democrats as always was to use their strengths to the maximum effect to outduel the GOP in getting more of its supporters, and that included many who chronically didn't vote, to the polls backing Democrats. Midterms would almost always be an uphill fight for the president's party. But they didn't have to be a fight that it was inevitable that his party would completely lose despite all the scare talk of wipeouts for the president's party.

There was always room in politics for surprises.

.

7

Warring on Voting Rights

"What Congress and the president do over the next several months is going to determine the fate of our Democracy." Mike Sozan's blunt quip about Congress and the president's action or inaction that could save or imperil democracy in the midterms was not mere hyperbole. Sozan, an official of the Center for American Progress, directly tied this concern to the 2022 midterms. He warned that the lack of congressional action on legislation languishing in Congress in April 2022 that would strengthen the Voting Rights Act and by extension voting rights would be catastrophic for the country, and especially for the Democrats.

Without congressional passage of Voting Rights Act amendments that restored some of the remedies that guaranteed the vote to all eligible voters, the grim prospect was yet another watered-down midterm voter turnout in 2022.

This was the great fear of Democrats. The legislation in question that concerned Sozan was two voting rights bills. *The Freedom to Vote Act* would expand mail voting, early voting, automatic voter registration, and curb partisan redistricting. The other bill was the John Lewis Voting Rights Advancement Act. It would reauthorize the 1965 Voting Rights Act.

Senate Minority Leader McConnell made clear that he opposed both bills. Every other GOP senator followed suit and either spoke out against the bills or remained silent. The reason was simple. The bills flew squarely in the face of the GOP's long game of gutting, eroding, and getting completely rid of the last vestiges of the landmark 1965 Voting Rights Act. The act did much to boost voter turnout from minority voters during the midterms. This benefited most Democrats.

The little drama that McConnell and GOP senators played out in stalling, if not killing, the Democratic-controlled House-approved voting rights enhancement bill was hardly surprising. It fit a pattern that had been well in place in opposing enforcement of the 1965 Voting Rights Act. The opening gun of the GOP war on the Voting Rights Act was sounded in the 1980s. Then-President Reagan invited a number of civil rights leaders to come to the White House on June 30, 1982, to witness his recertification of the 1965 Voting Rights Act. The provisions of the Act required congressional and presidential reapproval every 25 years to extend the provisions of the act.

The civil rights leaders were deeply concerned that Reagan given his virtual undeclared war with civil rights leaders over everything from opposition to affirmative action to the gutting of civil rights provisions to his cozying up to GOP Southern ultra-conservatives might delay or even refuse to sign the Voting Rights Act extension. Reagan had once called the Act "humiliating to the South." As for signing the extension, he had said virtually nothing about his intention.

However, his Attorney General William French Smith had plenty to say about the extension. He strongly urged Reagan to take measures to weaken provisions of the Act. The main one was to let the South off the hook on the requirement that it get Justice Department approval for elections in areas that have had a dubious history of voter discrimination. Failing that, Smith urged Reagan to strip down the Act. He didn't publicly at least specify what that meant. But the point was clear. Smith and other GOP conservatives close to Reagan weren't happy with the Voting Rights Act as it stood.

Reagan was having none of it. He signed the extension. However, he gave a veiled warning, "Yes, there are differences over how to attain the equality we seek for all our people." NAACP president Benjamin Hooks caught the drift of Reagan's warning and noted that he "belatedly" supported the measure and then added, "I don't think it indicates any change of heart at all. The Justice Department has systematically rolled back enforcement of civil rights legislation."

John R. Lewis
Voting Rights Advancement Act of 2021

Long title
An Act to amend the Voting Rights Act of 1965
to revise the criteria for determining which States
and political subdivisions are subject to section 4
of the Act, and for other purposes

It was an eerie Deja vu 25 years later on July 27, 2006, when then President Bush Jr. invited another coterie of civil rights leaders and congressional Democrats to the White House for his signing of the extension of the VRA. As with Reagan, there was some drama or rather pointed opposition to it. The same clique of Southern GOP conservatives and some Bush administration officials pulled the same page from the game plan they used with Reagan a quarter-century earlier and urged Bush not to sign the extension or demand some "modification" of the Act. They used the by now standard argument that it was unnecessary and was punitive to the South. Some even threatened to delay or even block passage in Congress.

A core of House Republicans did follow through on their threat to stall renewal. For more than a week, they dragged their feet on the legislation and demanded that hearings be held. They used the same old argument that it punishes the South for past voting-discrimination sins. They also didn't like the idea of bilingual ballots.

Bush as with Reagan ignored them and signed off on the extension in the White House ceremony. But Bush and Reagan's signatures on the Act's extension did nothing to quiet the war hoops from conservatives to gut the Act if not outright scrap it.

* * * * *

Seven years later conservatives finally had their long-held fond dream. They had a conservative majority on the SCOTUS. Even better, the newly installed SCOTUS Chief Justice John Roberts in 2005 was the one jurist who had protested the longest against the VRA. During those decades, Roberts canonized every argument that packs of GOP vote fraud adherents would self-righteously repeat. The VRA was an antiquated, outdated measure that no longer served the purpose for which it was originally needed. Robert's vendetta against the Voting Rights Act began in 1981.

That was the year Attorney General Smith advised Reagan to go slow on signing the VRA. The idea was the brainchild of one of his legal aides, none other than the then 26-year-old John Roberts.

In a memo to Smith, Roberts noted, "Something must be done to educate the Senators on the seriousness of this problem." He was emphatic, branding the Act, "constitutionally suspect." Even before Roberts began his assault on the Voting Rights Act, there were warning signs of trouble ahead. Some years earlier Nixon floated the idea of eliminating the preclearance provision which was the centerpiece of the Act that gave the Justice Department the right to intervene in elections deemed discriminatory.

It quickly died after an outcry from civil rights organizations. Yet that was just the opening gong for the assault. There were more court decisions in the early 1980s that gnawed away at the Act. In each case, the decisions raised the legal bar practically to the roof in now requiring the plaintiffs to prove that there was a "racially discriminatory motivation" in an election before bringing a discrimination lawsuit or challenge.

Congressional Democrats at that point held a comfortable majority in Congress. There was also still a core of moderate Republicans in the House and Senate. They beat back all efforts to water down the VRA. They enacted an amendment that banned any voting practice that "resulted in a denial or abridgment of the right of any citizen of the United States to vote on account of race or color."

Enter Roberts, he blitzed the Reagan officials with more than twenty-five memos imploring Reagan to greenlight the Justice Department to fight passage of the amendment.

Edward Blum, a wealthy anti-civil rights activist who would go on to be the driving force behind the Supreme Court case that gutted the preclearance requirement in

2013, complained in a 2006 *National Review* article, "Republicans don't want to be branded as hostile to minorities, especially just months from an election." Blum and other GOP opponents of the VRA bided their time until that fear had dissipated and there was a more politically favorable conservative climate in the country.

By 2013 there was. The SCOTUS agreed to hear the infamous federal lawsuit by Shelby County, Alabama that had quietly worked its way up through the appeals courts. The county wanted much of the Act dumped and recycled the same old arguments that it was outdated, discriminatory, and a blatant federal intrusion into state's rights. In times past, this claim would have gone nowhere.

But in 2013 the SCOTUS now had a conservative majority. Meanwhile, attorneys general in several states endorsed the Alabama county's challenge. And when then-Attorney General Eric Holder announced that he'd vigorously enforce all provisions of the Voting Rights Act to prevent voter suppression, that ignited more fury from the GOP. The predictable happened. The SCOTUS struck down the provision that especially riled the GOP. The provision mandated prior federal approval of changes to voting procedures in parts of the country with a history of racial and other discrimination.

The parts were the South and the Southwest. The heavy-handed discrimination targets were Black and Hispanic voters whose numbers were growing. The result of those growing numbers was that states in the South and

Southwest that had long been locked in the GOP vote column were now from the GOP's standpoint in danger of flipping to the Democrats.

＊ ＊ ＊ ＊ ＊

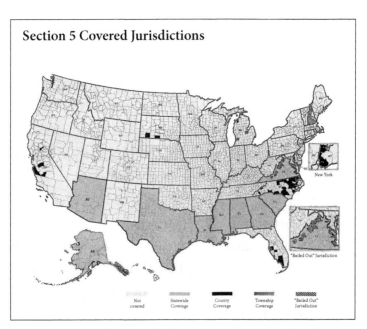

Note: Fifteen political subdivisions in Virginia (Augusta, Botetourt, Essex, Frederick, Green, Middlesex, Pulaski, Roanoke, Rockingham, Shenandoah and Warren counties and the cities of Fairfax, Harrisburg, Salem and Winchester) have "bailed out" from coverage pursuant to Section 4 of the Voting Rights Act. The United States consented to the declaratory judgement in each of those cases.

Source: U. S. Department of Justice, Civil Riights Division, Geographic Information Systems, Washington, D.C., January 17, 2008.

As originally enacted, the Voting Rights Act required jurisdictions with a history of racist voting discrimination to "preclear" any new voting-related laws with the Justice Department or with federal judges in Washington, DC. But this preclearance provision was initially scheduled to expire five years after the law was signed in 1965.

In 1970 Nixon was president. Congress that year had to decide whether to extend the preclearance requirement or allow it to expire. And, because Congress never made the preclearance requirement permanent, Congress also chose to extend this requirement again in 1975, 1982, and 2006. The GOP as is known undermined the Act with the rash of photo identification laws that the GOP governors and GOP controlled state legislatures enacted. They had one aim, and that was to discourage and damp down the number of minority and poor voters that overwhelmingly vote Democratic.

Despite the solid bipartisan support that the Act got in prior congresses and from GOP presidents, the Act has always been more controversial than many have believed.

The popular myth is that congressional leaders were so appalled and enraged at the shocking TV clips of Alabama state troopers battering civil rights marchers in Selma in March 1965 that they promptly passed the landmark law that restored voting rights to Southern Blacks. What's forgotten is that the marchers were there in the first place because the bill was badly stalled in the Senate and the House. It took nearly five months to get the bill passed.

Then Senate minority leader, Illinois Republican Everett Dirksen, heaped amendments on the bill that included scrapping the poll tax ban, adding exemptions and escape clauses for Southern counties, and excluding all states outside the South. House Republicans tacked more amendments on the bill to weaken it. The fight over these amendments dragged on for weeks in Congress.

* * * * *

In 2012 the GOP's legal assault on the Voting Rights Act shifted to the SCOTUS. Roberts was now in the legal driver's seat as SCOTUS Chief Justice. Given his avowed long history of antipathy to the Act, he left the heavy lifting to SCOTUS ultra-conservative Antonin Scalia during the court's oral arguments in Shelby County v. Holder (2013). He didn't disappoint, "I don't think there is anything to be gained by any Senator to vote against continuation of this act," Scalia continued. "And I am fairly confident it will be reenacted in perpetuity unless—unless a court can say it does not comport with the Constitution."

The court decision wiping out the preclearance provision, hated by the white South and GOP conservatives, was the crowning moment for Roberts. This supposedly proved his long-time argument that America had long since outgrown the dark days of Jim Crow exclusion of Blacks from the polls and had long since entered a new age of racial egalitarianism. The proof of that supposedly was the thousands of Black and Hispanic elected officials up to and including an African American president.

Roberts loftily declared," Yet nearly a half-century after the Voting Rights Act first became law, the conditions that originally justified these measures no longer characterize voting in the covered jurisdictions." Black voter turnout "has come to exceed white voter turnout in five of the six states originally covered by Section 5."

Robert's myopic, rosy view of a supposed color-blind America did not go unchallenged on the bench. Ruth Bader Ginsburg in her dissenting opinion noted, "Throwing out preclearance when it has worked and is continuing to work to stop discriminatory changes is like throwing away your umbrella in a rainstorm because you are not getting wet."

The problem with all this was that even in the most horrific days of the Jim Crow racial freeze out of Blacks in the South, there was never a word in any of the laws, ordinances, legal tracts, or court rulings that mentioned race let alone Blacks or Hispanics as being the explicit target of the vote freeze out. The exclusion was formalized through hints, nods, and legal subterfuges.

However, the result was the same. No Blacks voted even without the law saying that they couldn't. Some legislatures immediately took the hint from the 2013 court decision and with warp speed piled on various voter suppression restrictive laws –again always careful never to mention race. On the surface, the laws appeared completely race-neutral.

* * * * *

A near textbook example of this con game was the much-contested North Carolina vote law the GOP controlled legislature, quickly rushed through after the high court decision in 2013. Its voter ID requirement only permitted voters to use "those types of photo ID disproportionately held by whites and excluded those disproportionately held by African Americans." As one expert witness testified, several forms of ID that could not be used to vote under the North Carolina law—including government employee IDs, public assistance IDs, and student IDs—"provide relatively greater access to IDs for African Americans."

It was no accident that states such as North Carolina were in the front ranks of those trying to take full advantage of the High Court's slash of the VRA. They are swing states and Black voters increasingly play a significant role in breaking the GOP stranglehold on state, local and congressional offices in those states. This was especially important in the midterms where many congressional seats were hotly and keenly contested and where a relative handful of votes could swing the contest to one or the other candidate.

Ratcheting down the number of Black voters in these states struck a major blow to Democrats' effort to grab more state and federal offices in the midterms. This would shift the political power equation. No surprise, though, that when a federal appeals court struck down the North Carolina voting law, the Roberts High Court quickly upheld the law.

Roberts would never be satisfied until the Act was history. In one of his avalanche of earlier memos hammering the Act, Roberts wrote, "Voting rights plaintiffs can rely on the historical background of official actions, departures from normal practice, and other indirect evidence in proving intent. The Supreme Court has made clear that intent in this area ... may be proved by both direct and circumstantial evidence."

This was always the prime conservative fallback argument, namely, prove intent. To prove any discrimination no matter how outlandish and evident simply producing numbers, charts, and the visible effect of the discrimination would never be enough. Short of getting into the head and minds of those who racially discriminate and proving they deliberately and knowingly "intended" to discriminate, it's a near impossibility to prove intent legally.

This was the legal fiction and absurdity that Roberts operated under and when a voting discrimination case came before his court that would be the high bar he'd demand. Good luck on reaching that bar, given again the near impossibility of proving intent in discrimination cases, a fact Roberts well-knew.

Robert's High Court emboldened the GOP-controlled legislatures and GOP governors to enact their rash of voter restrictive laws. They were secure in the knowledge that even when a federal appeals court struck a restrictive law down, they had a near-fail safe backstop in the Roberts High Court. The protective shield was applied even when there were towering questions about how the ballots were counted in an election.

There was more. The Court's Republican majority, in

an unsigned opinion joined by Roberts, held that many ballots in which there was any question of an irregularity must be trashed. The crux of the Court's decision in *Republican National Committee v. Democratic National Committee* (2020) was that it was more important to prevent courts from altering "the election rules on the eve of an election" than it was to ensure that every vote is counted. It made absolutely no difference that tossing the ballots disenfranchised thousands of voters. It took little imagination to guess just who most of these disenfranchised voters were likely to be.

* * * * *

Despite their best obstructionist efforts, there was one thing that Robert and his SCOTUS conservative majority cohorts couldn't stop. That was the election of Democratic Joe Biden in 2020. Nor could they stop the election for the first time practically in living memory of two Democratic senators in a special election in January 2021 in what had been for decades solid Red State Georgia

Their win gave Biden a paper-thin majority in the Senate. The election, though, was the red flag for the GOP. The shock of losing the state to Biden and then followed by the even greater shock of losing two GOP-held Senate seats in the run-off race to Democrats was too much for the party to stomach.

The GOP need not have worried. It put its most reliable legal weapon at work again to further undermine the Act.

There was special urgency this time since the 2022 midterms were fast approaching. In June 2021, the SCOTUS struck. It upheld two clear vote suppression provisions passed by the GOP-controlled Arizona state legislature that virtually wiped out any chance for minorities in the state to challenge discriminatory voting restrictions.

One required that a ballot cast at the wrong precinct be trashed. The other is that only certain designated individuals can deliver another person's ballot to the polls. The provisions supposedly were a response to Trump's non-stop harangue that vote fraud robbed him of the White House in 2020. The provisions supposedly were measures to prevent the alleged fraud. A federal appeals court had earlier made clear that the provisions were nothing more than acts that ignored the "long history" of discrimination against American Indians, Hispanics, and African Americans.

The provisions hit hard at the two areas in the voting process that hampered minority voters. They were far more likely than whites to have their polling places switched, eliminated, or not receive any information on their placement before an election. American Indians and Hispanics, particularly new voters, were more likely to depend on others to deliver their ballots or cast absentee ballots. The provisions were vote suppression measures that on the surface seemed reasonable and tame enough

* * * * *

Biden saw it quite differently. He had one eye firmly on

the 2022 midterms. He realized the SCOTUS ruling could have a chilling effect on voting rights, "After all we have been through to deliver the promise of this Nation to all Americans, we should be fully enforcing voting rights laws, not weakening them."

The greater danger was that the SCOTUS would toss completely the other provision of the Act which has also been a major sore point for the GOP. That's section 2. It permits legal challenges to racial discrimination in voting procedures. The elimination of this section would for the last time erase from the books, the 1965 Voting Rights Act.

Meanwhile, though, the instant the Supreme Court seriously weakened the Voting Rights Act in 2013 by knocking out the key provision requiring Justice Department pre-clearance before a locale can alter or institute new voting procedures, the call went up for Congress to restore some version of this requirement. Then-President Obama and then-Attorney General Holder quickly added their voices to that call. The chances of that happening would always be zero if the GOP had its way. For most of the subsequent years when the GOP controlled Congress that's exactly what happened on voting rights, nothing.

The Supreme Court ruling on the VRA was a dream come true for the GOP. It accomplished in one fell swoop what GOP leaders for the past three decades strongly hinted they wanted to be done and that was to whittle down the landmark 1965 Voting Rights Act to the point of irrelevancy. It floated several trial balloons in Congress in

1981 and again in 2006 when the Act came up for renewal both times. Presidents Reagan and Bush Jr. signed the extension. Yet, in 2022, McConnell and GOP senators proved they could stall anything that strengthened voting rights by doggedly opposing the proposed amendments proposed by Democrats that enhanced voting rights.

* * * * *

Since the Act's inception, the GOP never wavered from its argument. That was that the Act punished the South for its history of blatant voting discrimination. But that past, the GOP claimed, was just that, the past, and the proof was the thousands of Black and Hispanic state and local elected officials from the South and Southwest and the millions of Black and Hispanic voters that were on the rolls in those states. The Supreme Court bought this argument. The Court majority deliberately ignored two glaring facts.

One was the well-documented sneaky ways that local registrars devised ploys to limit or eliminate minority voters. The other was the wave of voter suppression laws that GOP governors and GOP-controlled state legislatures plopped on the books during the past few years to shoo Black and Hispanic voters from the polls.

Even though Black and Hispanic voters did vote in big numbers in the 2012, 2016, and 2020 elections, in many districts they still had to stand in endless lines, have their IDs thoroughly scrutinized, had no bilingual ballots, found voting hours shortened, and had to file legal challenges in state and federal courts to get injunctions to stop the more onerous of the voter suppression laws from being enforced. The same rigid rules, scrutiny, and requirements were applied in the 2010, 2014, 2018, and 2022 midterms to minority voters to drive down their vote numbers.

The GOP vote suppression ruses for the most part fell flat on their face in 2012 and again in 2020 when Black and Hispanic voters ducked around the fresh barriers put up and jammed the polls in near-record numbers. They provided the numbers that insured President Obama's reelection by a comfortable margin. They also provided the margin that insured Biden's win over Trump in 2020.

Two years earlier, in the 2018 midterms, despite the formidable vote hurdles, the Black vote proved crucial to the Democrats flipping the House. The overall turnout nearly matched the record-high turnout of fourteen percent in the 2014 midterm.

A post-2018 midterm survey by the NAACP in collaboration with the Advancement Project and the African American Research Collaborative provided a revealing snapshot of what and why the turnout was again so high. It confirmed what many analysts noted, and Democrats fervently hoped. This was that the election would be a referendum on Trump. To be even blunter, that millions would act on their view of him as a supreme bigot and inflammatory hate monger and vote in massive numbers against the danger he posed. It found just that:

- 90% of Black voters supported Democratic House

candidates, compared to just 53% of all voters; 45% of white voters; 73% of Latinos; and 72% of Asian voters

- 72% of Black voters believe the Democrats are doing a good job with regards to the Black constituency, but 21% feel the Democrats don't care too much about Blacks.
- Only 12% of Black voters believe the Republicans are doing a good job with regards to the Black constituency, and 55% feel the GOP doesn't care too much about Blacks.
- 85% of Black women and 81% of Black men have felt disrespected by Donald Trump.
- Only 8% of Black voters believe Trump has a positive impact on Blacks, and 29% believe he has a negative impact.
- 89% of Black women, 83% of Black men, and 50% of white voters believe Trump's statements and policies will cause a major setback for racial progress
- 91% of Black women, 86% of Black men, and 50% of white voters believe Trump and the GOP are using toxic rhetoric to divide the nation
- 82% of Black women, 76% of Black men, and 45% of white voters believe Trump and the Republicans are normalizing sexism and sexual harassment against women.

The GOP managed to maintain its grip on the five Deep South states, and other Old Confederacy states in the 2012, and 2016 presidential elections. Though Georgia defected to Biden in 2020, the GOP still had a solid grip on the state legislature and governorship in the state.

The GOP performed superbly in the 2010, 2014, and even 2018 midterms. It did it as in the past almost exclusively with most of its votes coming from white voters. The increased number of Blacks and Hispanics in the states posed a mortal threat to continued GOP dominance in those states. That is if there were no barriers propped up to their registering and voting. Unfortunately, the Democrat's success in the 2018 midterms did not remove the dire threat that the mountain of voter suppression laws posed.

This is exactly why the GOP relied heavily on the Supreme Court dumping the crucial provision in the Act that insured a fair voting process. GOP leaders also knew that once the conservative Court majority ruled in its favor that some Democrats in Congress would certainly move to make over the law. They were right.

One obvious way the Democrats zeroed in on was to broaden out the pre-clearance provision to include other areas of the country that have had or could have potential voting restriction issues and then ensure that those jurisdictions be targeted for mandatory Justice Department monitoring. This would remove from the table the GOP's ancient contention that the Act unfairly targeted the South and some sections of the Southwest. This would easily pass constitutional muster since it would not single any one district, region, or state for restrictive monitoring or Justice Department litigation.

Even this practical remake of the disputed parts of the Act was anathema to the GOP. If proposed, GOP congressional leaders would dither, delay, and loudly squeal again that voter discrimination was non-existent. And that there was no need for adding another burdensome provision to the Voting Rights Act. This was exactly what the GOP House members did. Even though they were a minority in the House in 2021. Not one voted for HR 1. The bill would have restored and enhanced voting rights protections.

Yet, five conservative SCOTUS judges nullified what two GOP presidents, Reagan and Bush Jr., and Congress with overwhelming bipartisan support for more than a half-century routinely did. That was to ensure that the much fought for and prized Voting Rights Act stays in some form on the books guaranteeing that a fair, equitable, and democratic voting process remains the law of the land.

Meanwhile, the 2022 midterms were widely regarded as one of the most crucial midterms in decades. Maybe rivaling in importance, the 1862 midterms which was a political life and death referendum on Lincoln's administration, slavery, and the course of the Civil War. The battle lines were drawn tighter than ever in 2022 as in 1862.

The Democrats were determined to protect and expand voting rights. The GOP was equally determined to reduce them.

8

Destroying Two Presidents

"I'm really excited to be here tonight with the only group of Americans with a lower approval rating than I have." With that quip to the two thousand journalists and politicos at the annual White House Correspondents' Association dinner in April 2022, President Biden turned comedian for a moment. It was good Biden had a sense of humor about his plunging poll ratings. The 2022 midterms were at that point seven months away.

Biden well knew the disastrous history of midterm losses for the president's party. Anytime a president had poor ratings and the public frowned on him in the months before a midterm election, things usually went South for the president's party. Since the start of 2022, Biden's ratings had indeed tanked. Soaring gas prices, mounting inflation, the Russian-Ukraine war, and Biden's failure to deliver a convincing message about his legislative achievements, all worked to turn off big swatches of the public to his administration.

Biden knew that an invigorated, well-financed, and supremely confident GOP would work night and day to stoke the anger, frustration, and hostility of millions of Americans toward him in the months before the midterms. The GOP assault on a perceived vulnerable Democratic president was certainly not new. It was almost ritual. It took an especially biting, vicious, and take-no-prisoners turn in 2009. That year, the ringmaster of the GOP's hard-nosed attack plan was the party's top GOP political kingmaker, then GOP Senate Minority Leader Mitch McConnell.

"When I first came into office, the head of the Senate Republicans said, 'my number one priority is making sure president Obama's a one-term president.' Now, after the election, either he will have succeeded in that goal, or he will have failed at that goal," President Obama, interview on *CBS 60 Minutes,* recorded on September 12, 2012, and aired on September 23, 2012.

McConnell picked the perfect point to begin his assault on then-President Obama. It was the 2010 midterms. It was again a case of the GOP viewing the scoring of a big win in the midterms as the ideal weapon to blunt a Democratic president's legislative initiatives. McConnell wasted no words in an interview in the National Journal in October 2010, one month before the midterms. He told exactly what he planned to do to the Democrats but especially Obama in the 2010 midterms.

McConnell: "We need to be honest with the public. This election is about them, not us. And we need to treat this election as the first step in retaking the government. We need to say to everyone on Election Day. Those of you who helped make this a good day, you need to go out and help us finish the job."

NJ: What's the job?

McConnell: "The single most important thing we want to achieve is for President Obama to be a one-term president."

When the text of the interview was released, McConnell, and GOP apologists, quickly added that he didn't mean that he wanted Obama to fail. But that his words were designed purely as a bargaining chip to get Obama to adhere to the GOP's positions on the issues. McConnell ticked those issues off in a speech after the GOP had grabbed back the House and scored big gains in the Senate in the 2010 midterms:

"Let's start with the big picture. Over the past week, some have said it was indelicate of me to suggest that our top political priority over the next two years should be to deny President Obama a second term in office. But the fact is if our primary legislative goals are to repeal and replace the health spending bill; to end the bailouts; cut spending, and shrink the size and scope of government…"

McConnell did his homework. He tied the strategy of using the midterms as a weapon to render Democratic presidents politically impotent based on a study of the history of midterms when a president's party lost one or both houses of Congress. The lesson he claimed he learned from that history was to drill into the GOP troops and the public that the midterms were the absolute weapon to as he said of, "retaking the government." In other words, be open about the motives and that's the surest way to fire up voters.

* * * * *

In McConnell's eyes, the midterms weren't just an election, but a crusade. The crusading issue that he picked to open the attack on Obama, always with an eye on the midterms was the budget. The GOP and McConnell viewed this as Obama's and any Democratic president's political Achilles Heel. To hear McConnell and the GOP leaders tell it Obama had an alleged penchant for squandering tens of billions of taxpayer dollars on wasteful, nonproductive spending programs. McConnell even tossed in the GOP's favorite slur of Democrats when he lambasted Obama's budget proposals as "extra goodies for tax-and-spend liberals."

The added twist this time was that the GOP stood Obama's emphasis on middle-class job creation on its head and claimed that his budget proposals did absolutely nothing to create jobs and economic improvement for the middle-class. The aim was to tar Obama and the Democrats as big government, serial spending wastrels. The GOP peddled this line repeatedly to knock down any talk of a "grand bargain." This was a combination of tax increases on the wealthy in exchange for more and deeper spending cuts.

This was more GOP doggerel. Spending issues always played a significant role in the thinking of many economy-conscious voters in the months before the midterm elections. The 2010 midterms, therefore, were very much in the attack plans of McConnell and the GOP. The Democrats controlled both the House and Senate after Obama's sweeping White House win in 2008.

The GOP's only chance to torpedo Obama's legislative initiatives rested in snatching back one or both houses of Congress. The GOP deemed that picking a fight with Obama over the budget was the best weapon in its attack arsenal to make a case to the voters that the Democrats were again squandering taxpayer dollars.

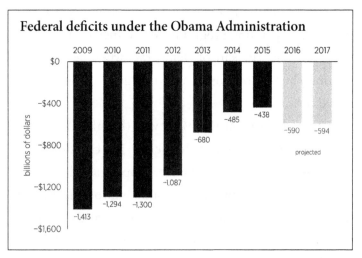

Source: CBO, "An Update to the Budget and Economic Outlook 2016 to 2026." Produced by Veronique de Rugy and Rizqi Rachmat, December 2016. Mercatus Center, George Mason University.

In prior budget proposals, Obama offered cuts to community service block grants which fund an array of community education, health, and social service programs in poor, underserved, largely inner-city neighborhoods, cut programs in science, technology, youth mentoring programs, and employment and training assistance. He even offered to tweak the GOP's prime slash and burn targets, Medicare, Medicaid, and Social Security.

The cuts to Medicare and Medicaid would have been stretched out over a decade and would have been no major structural reforms in the program, which is what the GOP demanded, and which was wildly at odds with the wish of most Americans. Many of them are dependent for their health coverage on the programs. But Obama still put the Medicare restructure proposals on the budget table, and they remained there.

Obama went even further and downplayed the surge in poverty that had dumped nearly fifty million Americans in or near poverty. Most without government subsistence programs were doomed to sink even deeper beneath the poverty line. This was not by choice. He was under relentless pressure from the GOP budget hawks and a sizable chunk of the public to make the cuts in these vital programs or risk sinking the federal government, so the GOP alleged, into a bigger pool of debt and deficit spending.

The topper was that the deficit in the 2010 midterm year would have fallen further and faster than at any point in the previous two decades. Obama with one eye on the midterms repeatedly agreed and pushed for a drop in the corporate tax and an overhaul of the tax system which if anything would have been even more business-friendly.

This was not enough to keep the GOP from stalling a budget deal. This was where the GOP's insidious motive came into play, namely naked, crass, go for the jugular politics. By embarrassing Obama at every turn on the budget, the GOP hoped to make him and the Democrats the perennial scapegoat for the budget gridlock. McConnell then could say to the voters in the midterms that Congress gets nothing done with a Democratic president and a Democratic majority Congress running the show.

The GOP's budget sparring match with Obama took an even more absurd turn when a pack of the most rabid House Republicans voted down a handful of spending proposals most notably on a transportation and housing appropriations bill that cut spending on programs in these areas. They claimed that even the reduced spending was still too high. This triggered a rarity, Republican infighting, in which one faction accused the other of "unrealistic and ill-conceived discretionary cuts." The result was that there was no new spending appropriation bill that Congress was likely to pass on a timely basis.

This delay also played into the GOP's hands. It further fueled the public impression that Congress was a tangle of gridlock and that the Democrats and Obama, were not only fiscal squanderers but were inept in getting congressional action on the most basic of fiscal policy initiatives, the budget passage.

When the GOP went after Obama on the budget it gave him little room to maneuver. Much of the public bought into the GOP's bogus line that Obama's alleged reckless spending was hopelessly drowning the government in a sea of red ink. Nervous foreign investors, as well as some financial experts and economists, endlessly claimed that the budget deficit—projected to soar higher to a post-World War II record—would saddle the nation, with higher taxes; greater cuts in education, health, and social services; staggering permanent debt; and even bankruptcy.

That doomsday scenario was part political hyperbole, and part financial panic. GOP operatives played hard on the alleged gloom and doom fiscal scenario. This was all designed to give the GOP a major edge in the 2010 midterms. It mattered little that many economists noted that the claim of financial Armageddon was overblown. The projected deficit was about 10 percent of the gross domestic product.

That would have been enough to threaten economic growth if it were sustained for decades. Yet even that supposed doomsday estimate was proportionally far smaller than the deficits that the United States ran during and immediately after World War II. That was never the point of the great dust-up over the budget. It was politics naked, and raw, with the crucial 2010 midterm election on the line.

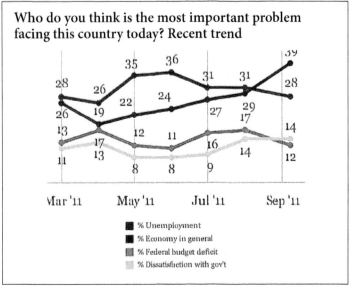

Source: Gallup

* * * * *

More than a decade later, the 2022 midterms were on the line. Biden realized the critical importance of the budget as a prime GOP campaign attack point. He sought to get out front on the issue. In March 2022, he announced his annual budget. The total was nearly six trillion dollars in spending. He especially wanted to outflank the GOP on the two issues that it would hammer him on with voters. They were crime and inflation.

The crime issue was particularly important for two reasons. One, crime, particularly violent crime, always touches a raw, emotional deep-seated fear in individuals. The other was that the GOP and conservative media steadily pounded a ferocious narrative throughout the latter part of 2021 and early 2022 that the nation was virtually under siege from violent criminals. They blamed the Democrats, painting them as advocates of defunding the police and for being soft on crime.

That was hardly the first time that a Democratic presidential candidate was snookered on the law-and-order scam by the GOP. Nixon kicked things off on this issue by tarring his Democratic opponent Hubert Humphrey in 1968 and the Democrats as soft on crime. George Bush Sr. worked the same angle with his Willie Horton hit ads on Democratic rival Michael Dukakis in 1988. The ads tarred Dukakis as soft on crime.

Trump snatched at the ploy in 2016 by grabbing every photo-op he could flanked by officials of various police unions. He promised to be the tough guy on crime. He came dangerously close to scrapping the rule of law and greenlighting any use of wanton force police use to crack down on crime. The issue proved to be a highly fertile field for Nixon, Bush Sr., and Trump. They won the White House. The consensus was that their stoke of public fear of crime, and gross misperceptions of who the violence mongers were, painting them as mostly young inner-city Black males, gave the GOP a huge edge with voters over their Democratic opponents.

Biden's counter was to up the ante in his budget in spending on police training, recruitment, and hiring to over $30 billion. Biden wasted no words in issuing a White House statement on why crime was a, if not, the pivotal issue in his budget.

"President Biden's fiscal year 2023 Budget calls on Congress to deliver the funding needed to implement the President's comprehensive strategy to reduce gun crime and make our communities safer. At DOJ alone, the President's Budget calls for $20.6 billion in discretionary funding for federal law enforcement and state and local law enforcement and crime prevention programs, an increase of 11% over FY22 enacted ($18.6 billion) and 18% over FY21 enacted ($17.5 billion). This funding will fund the police, including by putting more police officers on the beat, and make essential investments in crime prevention and intervention."

Biden's budget boost for the cops echoed his earlier address in March 2022, "We should all agree: "The answer is not to defund the police. It's to fund the police. Fund them. Fund them. Fund them with resources and training."

He didn't stop there. He made a beeline in March 2022 to New York City after a series of well-publicized shootings in the city to garner maximum media attention to his tough-on-crime and gun violence stance. A stern-faced Biden told reporters,

"Enough is enough because we know we can do things about this," Biden said. "But for the resistance, we're getting from some sectors of the government and the Congress and the state legislatures and the organizational structures out there, you know, Mayor Adams, you and I agree, the answer is not to abandon our streets, that's not the answer."

The GOP was quick to pounce on him and the Democrats. They pilloried him and them with the same attack line. Republican National Committee Chair Ronna Mc-Daniel led the charge, "Joe Biden and Democrats' soft-on-crime policies have emboldened criminals in Democrat-run cities across the country. Americans are less safe because of Democrats' failed leadership, and until Joe Biden condemns dangerous policies and anti-police rhetoric from Democrats like Manhattan District Attorney Alvin Bragg, he is complicit in the crime surges across the country."

Other Democrats, especially those in the must-win swing states, followed suit. They took great pains to denounce any call for defunding the police. One glance at the polls in early 2022 told how fraught the danger was for Democrats to be viewed as crime softies. Tw0-thirds of Americans opposed the defunding of the police call.

In mid-2022, crime was still very much on the minds of most Americans. One survey even rated it as the runaway number one concern of the public. The results of local and state primaries in a handful of states in June 2022 left no doubt about that. In the two cities, Los Angeles, and San Francisco, stout liberal, and Democrat-run cities that Biden won by lopsided margins in the 2020 presidential election, voters delivered their verdict on crime fears.

They propelled a former Republican and billionaire, Rick Caruso, into a run-off contest with stalwart liberal Democratic congressperson Karen Bass. Caruso got the backing of the Los Angeles Police Protective League and made safe streets, one of the cornerstone pledges of his campaign.

In San Francisco, voters by a big margin recalled liberal, reform-minded District Attorney, Chesa Boudin. His alleged sin, he was perceived as too soft on criminal prosecutions.

The crackdown on crime message from voters in the June primaries wasn't lost on Biden. He immediately returned to the crime issue to again try and outflank the GOP. "I think the voters sent a clear message last night: Both parties ought to step up and do something about crime, as well as gun violence. "The first major bill we passed, we gave the states and localities billions of dollars, billions of dollars, and encourage them to use it to hire police officers and reform their police departments. Very few have done it."

"It's time the states and the localities spend the money they have to deal with crime, as well as retrain police officers, as well as provide for more community policing. It's time to get on with doing that.

Biden was bound and determined not to let the GOP take sole ownership of the tough-on-crime line. However, the inescapable fact was that the tender box issue was still hurting Democrats, and that could well ultimately include Biden too.

* * * * *

Inflation fears ran close behind the crime scare as a major issue with voters in the months before the 2022 midterms. Biden understood that if voters felt that if the future looked glum for them financially, they'd seek someone to blame. That someone was the man in the White House and his party in the midterms. The GOP banged the drum hard on that. They finger-pointed Biden and the Democrats alleged profligacy on spending as the real cause of soaring prices. "Biden's reckless spending caused inflation," Republican Pennsylvania Senate candidate Mehmet Oz, noted in a campaign ad in March 2022.

This line came straight out of the RNC's midterm playbook to pulverize the Democrats on the nerve-wracking issue of the economy. Unfortunately, for Biden in May 2022, things hadn't improved much on the inflation front. A *CNN* poll that month found that it was by far the one issue that mattered most to voters.

The Russia-Ukraine war was a far, far distant second as an issue of concern in the poll. What was even more troubling for Biden, inflation worries cut across nearly every voter demographic—whites, Blacks, Hispanics, Asians, and those both over and under-aged 45 were troubled by the soaring costs. The even more startling finding was the roaring speed that which inflation had become an issue.

A year earlier most Americans said they thought the economy was in decent shape and felt fairly secure financially. Now in almost every case, respondents who said the economy was in bad shape pointed the blame finger at Biden. Or more specifically, they viewed his economic policies as the prime culprit for the nation's economic woes.

It was no surprise then that, yet another poll in April 2022 found that far more said the GOP could do a much better job handling the economy than Biden and the Democrats. This fed directly into the long-standing GOP attack point against the Democrats. That they spent, spent, and spent, and eventually that spending would wreak havoc with the economy, by piling up debt, and more debt. The GOP antidote was always the same, cut, cut, and more cuts. It rammed that message home with voters every chance it got before the midterms.

Of course, the GOP would carefully omit that there were major economic downturns, even collapse, and near collapse, under GOP administrations from Herbert Hoover through Bush Jr. But when control of Congress was on the line in a midterm election short memories, blatant omissions, and overblown historic distortions, would always be the order of the day.

Here's a sixty year look at early midterm voter preferences:

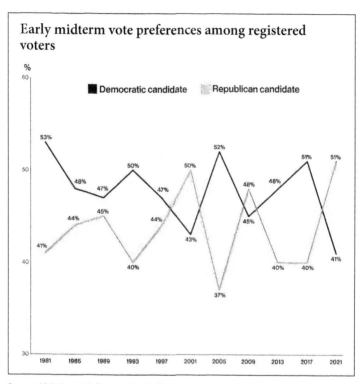

Source: ABC News/Washington Post Polls

The GOP twisted and mangled Biden's proposal to add billions to the 2022-2023 budget for the police as well as his repeated pledge to combat inflation as the days got closer to the midterms. It would smudge him and the Democrats as either not doing enough to deal with crime, and inflation, or spending too much which allegedly fueled inflation. The GOP budget assault was merely a rehash of the attack plan it used against Obama in the 2010 midterms. The difference this time was the GOP tossed in the two always touchy and thorny issues of crime and inflation to its assault.

* * * * *

The budget battle was only the latest issue the GOP grabbed at to prick Biden's alleged vulnerabilities with the voters. Not a moment had passed since he took office that somebody, somewhere wasn't making a political doomsday prediction that Biden would fail. There were endless stories about how he and the Democrats were in trouble and would lose big in the November 2022 primaries. Biden's plunged approval ratings were endlessly cited as proof of his and Democrat's supposed pending political fall.

This was the same template that the GOP and conservative media used during virtually every moment of the Obama presidency. That was to create a strawman argument that Obama's policies were a failure. That he could get few if any political initiatives through, and those he did get through such as the Affordable Care Act were bad. McConnell didn't get his dream of making Obama a "failure" and a one-term president. He simply switched gears and declared that he would make Obama's presidency a failed presidency.

The midterms again were his weapon of choice to make that happen. The GOP took back the House in 2010. McConnell pulled out all stops to finish the job in the 2014 midterms. When he did, and the GOP took back the Senate to go with its control of the House it won in the 2010 midterms, a beaming McConnell issued a stark warning to Obama, "don't poison the well." The poison he meant was

Obama not heeding the midterm results and bulling ahead with his agenda. By "well" McConnell meant the GOP's agenda.

The game plan was the same with Biden and the 2022 midterms. Play up big every supposed Biden misstep, gaffe, or policy fumble. At the midwinter meeting of the Democratic National Committee meeting in Washington D.C. in March 2022, as mentioned, Biden sounded the alarm. He warned Democrats to get doubly busy and get a massive Democratic voter turnout in November 2022. The loss of the House or the Senate or both would be catastrophic. It would guarantee that Biden's remaining two years of his first term would be neutered by the GOP.

McConnell and nearly all the GOP senators gave a preview of the hardball game they'd play with Biden after his nomination of Ketanji Brown Jackson for the SCOTUS in March 2022. The near-universal consensus was that she was one of the most eminently qualified jurists to come down the pike in years. Her confirmation as the first Black woman on the High Court would not just be a historic first, but also a neat, and fitting testament to the nation's diversity and commitment to racial equity.

McConnell and nearly all the GOP senators had other ideas. They hectored and impugned Jackson with every nonsensical, and plain silly question and assertion at her committee hearings. Then with three exceptions voted against her confirmation. Then with only one exception, Mitt Romney, they refused to even give polite applause when her confirmation was approved-mostly by Democrats. Nearly all of the GOP senators walked out.

McConnell and the GOP kicked things into even higher gear afterward by mounting a relentless and ruthless pre-midterm campaign of hectoring, harassing, dithering, diddling, and obstructing many of Biden's major initiatives. McConnell continued to have an almost united, lockstep GOP behind him. He was armed with total mastery of all the parliamentary and legislative tricks of the Senate trade to stonewall Biden.

Still, Biden held out some hope that he could work with McConnell and the GOP on at least some issues. If nothing else, by trying to reach across the aisle to McConnell, it would show he was making a good faith effort to restore some degree of bipartisanship to the Senate. Democratic Senate Majority Leader Chuck Schumer quickly disabused him of that notion. In a candid conversation with Biden, he told him that McConnell might pretend to be chummy with him at times, but he would still do everything he could to obstruct his agenda.

* * * * *

In the months before the midterms, Biden faced a continuing clean-up job. There was the COVID battered economy and continued worries about a still dangerous public health crisis, the soaring gas prices, and the lethal, and unpredictable course the Russian war against Ukraine could take.

Biden, though, scored some notable wins. He got an agreement between congressional Democrats and Republicans on a stimulus deal. He got his massive Build America infrastructure bill through.

However, he was quickly thrust into the brewing battle over the SCOTUS decision on *Roe v. Wade.* There was little doubt that the conservative majority on the court would dump *Roe* before its 2022 summer recess. The ultra-right had worked for decades in the courts and GOP controlled state legislatures to put the severest restrictions possible on abortion. It took years but they now had the committed votes on the High Court to finish their quest for overturn. The pending scuttle of *Roe* ignited a public firestorm on both sides of the battle lines on this perennially hyper volatile issue.

There were two pressing questions on this penultimate polarizing issue. The first was what would Biden say and do. In May 2022, a month, before the decision was rendered, he said what was expected," woman's right to choose is fundamental, *Roe* has been the law of the land for almost 50 years, and basic fairness and the stability of our law demand that it not be overturned." As for what he'd do, he tossed it back to Congress and the Democrats, to first elect more pro-choice senators and representatives, and then pass legislation protecting abortion rights.

The second question related to his call for more pro-choice congressional representatives. That was would the overturn of *Roe* by a right-wing High Court, help the Democrats fire up their supporters to rush to the polls in the

2022 midterms to elect those pro-choice House members and senators Biden called for?

As always, there was endless guesswork about whether scrapping *Roe* would give Democrats the made-in-heaven weapon to energize en masse their supporters and millions more who supported a woman's right to choose. The early returns showed that it was the silver bullet issue for the Democrats. In a poll in April 2022, respondents were asked, "What effect do you think *Roe v. Wade* being overturned would have on November's Congressional elections?" The overwhelming majority said not only would it help the Democrats but that the abortion decision would determine their vote.

There was a cautionary note to this. The poll and the SCOTUS decision on *Roe* came five months before the midterms. That was a lot of time in between for the GOP to rally and sell its supporters that the court made the right decision and that it was just as important for them to hit the polls to show their support for anti-choice GOP incumbents and candidates. The decision gave both sides ammunition for the midterms.

On another matter, McConnell, and the GOP, fortunately, couldn't fully do to Biden what they did to Obama. That was to completely hamstring him on the confirmation of his nominations and appointments to federal courts and administration posts. But only because the confirmation process was by a simple majority. Democrats for the moment still had a razor-thin Senate majority.

Yet, there was an array of housing, education, foreign policy, and spending decisions that were on the table. Biden would be forced to sign off on a rash of executive orders on education reforms and enhanced environmental and consumer financial protections. These were reforms Obama penned by executive order and Trump moved quickly to try and wipe them out. Whenever Biden had to use his executive pen, he evoked the same howls Obama got from McConnell and the GOP that he was a tyrant and dictator and abused the power of his office by usurping Congress.

* * * * *

There was the issue of criminal justice reform and voting rights protections. Biden walked a continuous tightrope on these issues. He was pushed hard by Black Lives Matter, criminal justice reform advocates, and civil rights groups to make good on his promises for reforms in community policing, police-community relations and to rein in police abuse. This stirred a fierce backlash from police unions and conservatives that he encouraged lawlessness and weakened law enforcement. He backed far away from any advocacy of defunding the police. It was the prudent, almost mandatory move to make since polls continued to show many Americans wanted more not less spent on public safety.

The Democratic-controlled House passed voting rights protection bill also remained a flashpoint of contention between Democrats and the GOP. There was little

Biden could do to move the bill to passage in the Senate. McConnell had effectively shut that down.

It was not a pretty picture for Biden as the days ticked down to the 2022 midterms. One that was made even uglier by the GOP and the conservative media. Biden was a skilled and seasoned politician though. He, like McConnell, knew the monumental stakes in the 2022 midterms for his administration and the Democrats. It would take all his skills and the firm backing of the Democratic party to keep the GOP from destroying his presidency in the midterms and beyond.

He could not afford an Obama repeat.

Conclusion
Midterm Lessons

Throughout the nation's history the midterms have had enormous consequences for both the president's party and the country. The jobs of lots of individual members of Congress, as well as the jobs of top members of the president's staff, were on the line. But more importantly, the control of the House and Senate by the Democrats or Republicans was up for grabs.

There were also innumerable state offices, legislatures, and governorships, which could change party hands in the midterms. Whichever party controls the House and or the Senate, would set the legislative agenda. They would get to pick committee heads, determine what bills are considered or scrapped, and the timetables for them. The greatest advantage the party in control has is that it can sabotage, dither, delay, ignore, or outright scrap the president's legislative initiatives.

A split in government with one party controlling Congress and the other controlling the White House makes for perennial gridlock, endless political posturing, and out and out political warfare. The control of the Senate is especially worrisome in any midterm election for a sitting president.

In 2022, the Democrats hung onto control by the barest margin. It would only take the flip of one Democratic senate seat in the midterms to the GOP to radically change the power dynamic in the Senate. Almost certainly McConnell would be back in the driver's seat as Senate Majority Leader if that happened.

One of the most crucial, if not the most crucial policy issue, that the Senate and by extension McConnell would be in a strong position to dictate on is a SCOTUS nomination. If Biden had the chance to nominate another SCOTUS judge during the last two years of his term, this would narrow down the ideological balance between the hardline conservative majority that dominated the court as of 2022 and the moderates on the bench.

McConnell would follow the same template that he did with Obama when he nominated Merrick Garland in March 2016 to the High Court. McConnell killed the nomination. He'd do the same with Biden's pick. This was not speculation. McConnell as much as said that in interviews in early 2022.

This is only one terrifying example of the power that a majority party can weld when in control of one or both wings of Congress. The midterms far more than the general election decide who controls what gets done in Congress as well as in many of the states.

A decisive win by either party in the midterms builds up political steam and their confidence for the presidential election two years following. Almost certainly, the GOP if they won congressional control in 2022 would scramble fast to find a compelling candidate to challenge President Biden in 2024.

Presidents always face one seemingly intractable problem with midterms. Their approval ratings. They often drop and they are closely watched as clues about how people feel about the President, his policies, and whether they like or dislike the direction the country is going in. The public mood and feelings—for good or ill- land rudely on the doorstep of the President and his party.

Unfortunately, for Biden, as was true for Trump and Obama, at the midpoint of his first term, the mood of many Americans had turned ugly. The 2014 and 2018 midterms showed that. Republicans took back the House in 2014 under the Obama regime. Democrats took back the House in 2018 under the Trump regime.

* * * * *

It's not solely a numbers game for the midterms. That is simply counting how many potential voters a party has. In terms of sheer numbers on paper, the Democrats have had a decisive edge over the GOP since the election of Obama in 2008. The real indicator of how the president's party will fare in midterms is the passion and enthusiasm of their and the opposition party's supporters.

This generally is the bellwether of who is most likely to show up at the polls in the midterms. Though Trump lost the White House in 2020, there were a couple of frightening clues that there was lots of passion for what he and the GOP represented.

The first was the sickening footage of the storming of the Capitol by Trump-instigated terrorists on January 6, 2021. No matter how ugly and illegal the storming, a parade of GOP senators flatly said that this was not enough for them to vote for a Trump conviction following his impeachment in the House—again. Their rally around the disgraced former President had nothing to do with personal or partisan dislike of the impeachment process aimed at one of their own. It was a matter of numbers, fear, and brutal political gamesmanship.

The seventy-four million votes Trump received in his losing White House bid in 2020 were the greatest number of votes a losing presidential candidate has ever gotten in a free election anywhere, ever. It was a greater number than any American presidential winner had gotten before. How Trump got those staggering numbers told much about why GOP politicians were buoyant about the 2022 midterms.

Nearly two dozen GOP senators would be up for reelection. Many still had fresh memories of a decade ago, when hard-right Republican activists' saber-rattled GOP senators, demanding they tow their political line, or they'd find a hard-rightist to run against them in the primary. Trump continued to play that game within the GOP in an early run-up to the 2022 midterms. In Michigan, he backed two hard-right candidates for state offices. Why? Because they backed his fraudulent claim that the 2020 presidential election was stolen from him.

No GOP incumbent wanted to sweat through that nightmare of having a hard right, pro-Trump-backed, opponent trying to oust them. The tens of millions of Trump backers loomed big in their terror of that happening.

Many believed Trump's frenzied backers were the GOP's life support. Any fall off the cliff from support from them meant kissing control of the Senate goodbye in the midterms. This would blow apart McConnell's long game of obstructing every major initiative of Biden and the Democrats.

Even if Trump had vanished in thin air overnight before the midterms it wouldn't alter the powerful, undeniable forces that propel American politics. So powerful that, despite the irrefutable proof that the 2020 presidential vote process was accurate and untainted, more than half of Republicans still claimed in 2022 that the election was stolen from Trump. They still spun every kind of ridiculous conspiracy theory about the alleged theft and made clear they'd never acknowledge the legitimacy of Biden's presidency.

Much is made that America will no longer be an old-white-guy-run country in 2050, that white male voters have steadily dropped in national elections, and that Blacks, Hispanics, Asians, women, and young persons will be the new majority voters. But in 2022 that was still a long way off. White males still had outsized voter clout in the crucial Heartland states and the South for the 2022 midterms and the 2024 presidential election.

Trump and the GOP knew that. This meant continuing to play hard on his base's latent racist, anti-immigrant, anti-woman pseudo-patriotic sentiment. Trump bullied and intimidated GOP leaders into believing that defying him spelled doom for incumbents in their reelection bids. That was the type of voter loyalty that buys a lot of support from the GOP establishment.

It would be missing too much to think that midterms are only about the like or dislike of the man in the White House. Issues and how they are framed and messaged figure mightily in the midterm calculus. In just about any midterm election the shape of the economy, and how bread and butter issues affecting the average American will propel the debate and the vote.

For the most part, the American economy has done fairly well in most years since World War II. Unemployment in midterm election years has been under 6 percent and the country's economic growth rate has been close to 2 percent. However, there's more to this than the numbers when assessing the importance of the economy and the midterms.

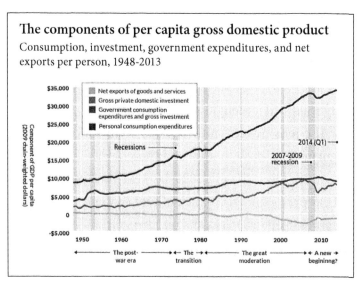

Source: Washington Center for Equitable Growth. Author's calculations using data from National Income and Product Accounts tables from the Bureau of Economic Analysis. Recession dates are from the National Bureau of Economic Research's Business Cycle Dating Committee.

* * * * *

The 2014 midterms were just one example of the dominant impact the economy has on voter perceptions of the president and ultimately voter turnout in the midterms. In a news conference in a run-up to that year's midterms, then-President Obama said, "The economy is stronger than it's been in a very long time." He was correct. The stock market was up. Unemployment had dropped and everything from auto sales to housing seemed to be booming. However, a good economy was the start not the end to determine just how that affected Americans and how they perceived the economic good times affected them.

Many people still didn't feel good about where they

were at in terms of their financial well-being in 2014. Despite the good economic numbers, the feeling was widespread that things weren't so good and could again downturn. The GOP pounded that message home. It worked. The party solidified its congressional takeover.

The jobs figures in early 2022 were superb. Unemployment continued to drop and those on the jobless roles were much lower than in 2021. However, surging inflation and gas prices undercut much of that economic buoyancy. Merely citing percentages and numbers meant little to most people.

What did mean something was when they went to the gas station and saw the soaring prices of a gallon of gas staring them in the face and had to pay double and triple more to fill up their cars. Or when they went to the market and had to pay double for what they paid for an item a year earlier. The economy then was not an abstraction, but a real, harsh, personal pocketbook concern.

Tied in with that is the cost of government. Almost always, Democrats remind voters that they are the party that fights to expand the economic and social safety net for working people and the poor. In the months before the 2022 midterms, Biden talked much about expanding the net even more with his support of programs such as universal prekindergarten, expanded Medicare services, and a big investment in combating climate change and extended child tax breaks to lift millions of children out of poverty. "This legislation presents the most historic and transformative agenda in a century," House Speaker Nancy Pelosi (D-Calif.) wrote to her colleagues in a letter in early 2022.

Meanwhile, the GOP almost always counters that talk by talking about how much those programs would cost workers and especially the middle class. The party protests that these programs are not just costly. They allegedly prove that the Democrats have an insatiable tax and spend mentality all at the expense of the taxpayer's purse.

The GOP went one better in the 2018 midterms. It tried to make them a referendum on Pelosi rather than Trump. The hope was that the widespread dislike of Pelosi in the Heartland states would drive GOP supporters to the polls. It didn't work then. However, there was nothing to stop the party from reprising that attack line in the 2022 midterms.

There was another curious feature to the 2022 midterms that was somewhat different than other midterms. In early 2022 polls, the Democrats and Republicans were in a dead heat in the number of voters that supported their party's positions on the issues. Forty-three percent of voters said they planned to cast ballots for the GOP congressional candidates. The same percentage said they would do the same for Democratic contenders.

The likelihood was that the dead even number of voters between the parties would hold to the midterms. That meant that both parties would have to do much more to woo more non-voters to the polls. The Democrats seemed to have a slight advantage. Polls consistently showed that those likely not to vote were lower-income, minorities, and young persons. This was the voter demographic that leaned heavily toward the Democrats if they voted.

The GOP recognized that. This was a major reason that GOP-controlled legislatures tried to erect every barrier they could think up to ratchet down the number of the voters that might register and vote. The assumption was that more of them would register and vote as Democrats than Republicans. They were right. "Non-voters are far more Democratic in their political leaning, more likely to favor activist government, including the health care legislation, and more likely to approve of Obama's performance in office," noted Scott Keeter of the nonpartisan Pew Research Center, which compiled a comparison of attitudes between 2010 voters and non-voters for ABC News.

This represented a plus for the Democrats that bumped up against the history and difficulty of turning non-voters into Democratic voters. With few exceptions, the turnout in nearly all midterms has been stuck at under fifty percent of eligible voters. The biggest wall to break through was a strong perception repeatedly voiced in interviews with non-voters that if it's not a presidential election, they did not consider it important enough to vote.

This was far from the truth. The major decisions that affect people's lives such as programs and spending on education, job creation, the environment, housing, and taxing are made or decided by Congress and state legislatures. Midterms in more instances than presidential elections often determine which party controls Congress and the state legislatures. Biden was clear on this in his remarks at the Democratic National Committee winter meeting in March 2022, "It's going to be a sad, sad two years. Think about it if Republicans controlled the Congress these last two years."

* * * * *

Sad or no, millions of Americans are unable to make the connection between midterm results and the control of the government. There is only one president, and one hundred senators and 435 House members, and tens of thousands of state and local legislative offices. It takes more than a scorecard to keep up with the numbers and the candidates for national state offices. In most cases, they are unknown, faceless, and seemingly inconsequential to many voters and non-voters. For others, the sheer numbers they must choose from in the midterms are overwhelming.

This doesn't change the harsh fact for Democrats that there were millions of voters who were likely to vote for a Democratic candidate or incumbent. Yet they routinely did not vote on midterm Election Day. Biden added even more to his quip about a sad two years if the GOP won the 2022 midterms, "It's going to be even sadder for Blacks and Hispanics."

Biden's point was well taken. He and the Democrats desperately needed a repeat of the 2018 midterms.

The chart tells why:

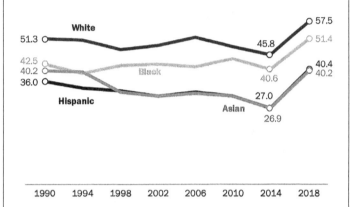

Note: Eligible voters are U.S. citizens ages 18 and older. Whites, blacks and Asians include only non-Hispanics. Hispanics are of any race.

Source: Pew Research Center analysis of the Current Population Survey, November Supplements, 1990-2018.S.

Still, memories lingered of the disastrous 2014 midterms. They loomed large as the gold standard of what a GOP takeover of Congress meant for minorities. Two weeks before the midterms, GOP pundits and some in the media gleefully noted that a few African American listeners purportedly walked out on President Obama during a campaign speech he made at a Maryland high school on October 19, 2014. Obama appeared at the school to boost the candidacy of Maryland gubernatorial Democrat candidate Lt. Governor Anthony Brown.

Brown was in a bid to become the nation's second African American governor. This was more than merely an excuse to poke fun at Obama. The point was that supposedly many African Americans were so turned off by Obama that they would stay home in droves on November 4, the day of the midterms. And since Black and Hispanic voters typically have a lower turnout during off-year national elections than older whites, this supposedly would further shatter the Democrat's chances of staving off the much-predicted Republican "wave" of mid-term election victories.

A standard prediction was that the GOP was likely to seize control of the Senate, tighten its grip on the House, and ramp up its control of even more state legislatures and possibly governorships. The GOP made no secret of what would happen if it did.

It would hammer even harder the Affordable Care Act, permanently shelve any effort at a minimum wage hike, kill any effort to strengthen voting rights protections, further stymie efforts to expand Medicaid, and harden its line against any of Obama's judicial and administration appointees that it deemed too liberal or moderate. It would effectively dismantle the firewall that Senate Democrats had erected to keep many of the nutty, retrograde initiatives and bills shoved up by the Tea Party-influenced GOP-controlled House from getting to the Senate floor.

This would force Obama to do two things to counter the GOP dominance. One was to veto any of the GOP passed bills that gutted or pecked away at his education, health care, and job creation spending and initiatives. The other was to force him to continue to pen more executive orders to get any effective action on vital initiatives. In both cases, the GOP stood this on its head and screamed even louder that Obama was a tyrant and attempting to usurp congressional authority. There were repeated dark hints of impeachment. The aim was to emasculate his presidency.

Then Senate Minority Leader McConnell crowed the day after Obama won the election in 2008 that the GOP would do everything humanly possible to make Obama either a one-term president or failing that a failed presidency. That boast wasn't just about stonewalling Obama. It was a continuation of the GOP's high-intensity war waged by successive GOP presidents Reagan, Bush Sr., and George W. Bush against the moderate reform agenda of Democrats. What's euphemistically called the liberal, big government, entitlement agenda. It meant an attempt to dismantle or gut the entire range of health, education, and economic support programs for the poor, working-class, and minorities.

For the last six years of Obama's White House tenure, the GOP controlled House, most GOP senators, and GOP controlled state legislatures and statehouses across the country, dithered, hectored, obstructed, and torpedoed the range of initiatives from voting rights protections, Medicaid expansion, greater public school funding, job creation programs, criminal justice, and immigration reform, blocked the appointment of moderate judicial nominees, and intensified the assault on labor unions and the Affordable Care Act.

A GOP compliant Supreme Court in 2010 did everything possible to demolish the campaign funding playing field to allow big corporations and Wall Street to bankroll with impunity rock-solid corporate and financial industry-friendly Republicans and some Democrats. In *Citizens United v. Federal Election Commission* ruling, it knocked out restrictions limiting the amount of dollars corporations could directly contribute to political campaign committees. The corporate money floodgate was now wide open.

* * * * *

The GOP's end game in the 2014 midterms was not just to finish the conservative counter-revolution, but to establish a winning game plan for the 2016 presidential election. It was a simple one, pass more vote restrictive laws to drive as many Blacks and Latinos from the polls as possible. Then pour tens of millions into an unprecedented campaign of lies, distortions, and all out-character assaults on Hillary Clinton in an effort to knock her out of the box as the Democrat's best hope to keep the White House.

The brutal reality was that a GOP-controlled Congress, a GOP White House, a lockdown conservative majority Supreme Court and a majority of GOP controlled state legislatures and governorships would pose something that America hadn't seen in decades. That was a GOP-dominated America. That was a scary prospect. The even scarier part was that many potential Democratic voters by not voting guaranteed that the dire prophecy of what would happen after the 2014 GOP congressional, and state legislative takeover came to pass.

In an interview on *CBS* a few days after the midterm drubbing, Obama acknowledged the obvious that the midterms were a referendum on him and his party,

"The buck stops right here at my desk. And so whenever – as the head of the party – it doesn't do well, I've got to take responsibility for it." His approval rating had sunk to a six-year low, and many Democratic candidates and incumbents were openly avoiding association with him.

Obama offered a thoughtful post-midterm assessment of what could have been done differently, "I think that one thing that I do need to constantly remind myself and my team of is it's not enough just to build a better mousetrap. People don't automatically come beating on your door. We've got to sell it, we've got to reach out to the other side and, where possible, persuade."

"I think that what you'll see is a constant effort to improve the way we deliver service to customers. So, there is a failure of politics there that we've got to improve on."

Obama then followed quickly with a national radio address on the midterms. He warned that the midterm losses were largely due to voter frustration, "They see Washington gridlocked and they're frustrated. And they know one person in Washington and that's the President of the United States." There, Obama said it, "Frustration" and "the President," these are the two combustible words that are welded together in the minds of millions that propel them to the polls to vote against the president's party or worse for his party, not to vote at all in the midterms.

* * * * *

In 2022, Biden was faced with the same dilemma and peril that Obama faced eight years earlier after the 2014 midterm losses. Biden, like Obama, understood the make-or-break importance of his presidency of the midterms. The midterms as in nearly all other midterms from the past could also hurt those who stood to gain the most from having more Democrats than Republicans in office. Both the GOP and the Democrats deemed millions of Americans to be their constituencies. Both parties claimed to speak for them. The midterms were and would always be their most important battleground

This can't be separated from one other crucial point about American politics. That is the right to vote is the foundational cornerstone of American democracy. When that right is under siege, the loser is not just American voters, but democracy.

The fierce battles over the midterms horrifyingly underscore that.

Postscript
The 2014 Versus 2022 Midterms

GOP strategists were ecstatic over the thought that they could snatch back the Senate and make even bigger gains in the House in the 2014 midterm elections. Their glee was fed by the glitches and snafus in the Obamacare rollout. In addition, the seeming freefall in the popularity ratings of President Obama, and the polls that showed more Americans favored the GOP on the budget and the economy than Democrats was cause for more GOP glee.

The GOP relied on getting the usual bigger turnout in the midterms of older, white voters. They would more than offset turnout from the Democrat's core voters—young persons, Blacks, Hispanics, and college-educated women voters. For the most part, they were implacably hostile to the GOP. One more GOP potential plus was the seemingly ritual congressional losses by the president's party in midterm elections.

If it were just a case of the GOP going head-to-head with Democrats, the rosy scenario would have played out as expected. But the Democrats' biggest ace card to stave off electoral losses in 2014 was the GOP. More specifically the Tea Party, which starting in 2010, was in its ascendancy. It still seemed to be riding high in 2012 when Obama won a convincing reelection bid.

There was little reason to think much would change in 2014. Most of the twelve Republican senators up for reelection drew Tea Party fueled challengers. In some cases, the Tea Party supported GOP Senate challengers got a financial boost from the influx of funds from conservative advocacy groups that were unabashed in proclaiming they wanted the GOP incumbents out.

In the days after the GOP got creamed in the 2012 presidential election, Tea Party leaders railed that the GOP had made its own badly ruffled election bed when it tried to be all moderate things to all people. The dilemma for the GOP establishment was that the continuing palace revolt by various Tea Party factions would hurt the GOP in the 2014 midterm elections.

The Tea Party, though, by 2014 was saddled with the baggage of being too far right, and too disruptive, to suit the taste of many. In 2012, polls showed that more Americans had an unfavorable view of the Tea Party than when it roared on the scene shortly after Obama's election in 2008. Every poll showed a continued rise in opposition to the Tea Party.

The alleged disaffection cut across all lines and included many conservatives. The reason for the decline in Tea Party backing in Red State districts wasn't hard to figure out. When Tea Party-affiliated candidates scored big victories and even upsets of GOP incumbents in some races in 2010, they had one mantra. That was to shrink government and shrink it fast. Millions of Americans cheered their war call and voted for the candidates that shouted it the loudest.

Yet it was one thing to scream about big government, bloated federal spending, and whopping-sized federal deficits. It was quite another to hold Congress, and by extension, the nation hostage in an uncompromising, shrill battle to chop down the government. The result was that Congress was at a virtual stall for two years and public approval of Congress dropped to lows that made used car salespersons look like public heroes.

The three big issues before the 2014 midterms that did much to plunge Tea Party support were the budget, immigration reform, and tougher gun control curbs. Nothing seemingly changed by 2014. The Tea Party still seemed wildly out of step with most Americans. Polls and surveys on all three issues then, especially gun control, found that most Americans wanted Congress to take immediate and decisive action to break the lethargy and stalemate on all three issues.

A drug out battle in Congress over these issues again appeared not to be in the public cards. GOP leaders viewed this kind of trench warfare as an absolute prescription for political disaster that played into the hands of Democrats. It allowed them to continue to lambaste the GOP as a hateful, vengeful party of nihilism and obstructionism. This was exactly what got the GOP into such deep hot water in the run-up to the 2012 presidential elections and party leaders saw how disastrous that was for the GOP.

Early in 2013, the Republican National Committee took another step to create the public appearance that the GOP was a reasonable, inclusive party, which stood for something other than bashing Obama. It made a cosmetic, PR leaden, effort to show that it learned its lesson from the 2012 election debacle. It issued a one hundred page plus manifesto on ways to broaden the appeal of the party. The manifesto was ridiculed and ignored by ultra-conservatives who clung hard to the notion that the salvation of the GOP was to move even sharper and faster to the hard right.

This would have been a prescription for electoral disaster in the 2014 midterms. Such a stance would have imperiled the GOP's object of completing its takeover of Congress which it had only partially obtained in the 2010 midterms when it captured the House.

Everything depended on the GOP slightly refashioning its image into one of it being a party that could get things done in Congress if it controlled it. The doubters among much of the public, wary of Tea Party extremism, had to believe that if the GOP were to triumph in the midterms. The strategy worked. GOP leaders distanced the party from its Tea Party connection, downplayed any racial animosity toward Obama, and mounted a devastating effective ground game that stirred its supporters and other voters to back GOP congressional candidates and incumbents. The 2014 midterms completely belonged to the GOP.

The grim 2014 Democratic Prospects for Holding the Senate:

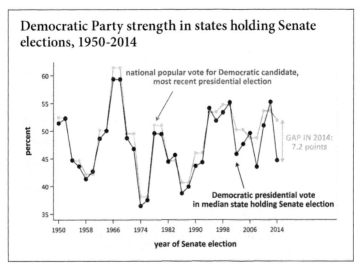

Note: Percentages are share of major-party vote.
Source: The Monkey Cage/Washington Post by Patrick J. Egan, NYU.

* * * * *

Fast forward nearly a decade to the 2022 midterms. The Tea Party was history. Biden's popularity numbers had dropped, and the GOP had two handmaiden issues—crime and inflation—to ring lots of political capital out of. Many polls, surveys, and an endless number of political analysts predicted months before the November balloting that the GOP would score big in the midterms.

The only real threat and spoiler to this idyllic midterm scenario was Trump. He again had shoved his way into some of the 2022 GOP primary races to back far out, ultra-right, borderline loon candidates against established viable GOP incumbents and candidates. This threatened to create chaos and division within the GOP in the run-up to the 2022 midterms.

The other issue that could throw a monkey wrench into the GOP's march to midterm victory was abortion. The SCOTUS's hard-right majority was expected to scrap Roe. That potentially could give Democrats a made-in manna issue to skewer the GOP as a party that warred on women and was run by an unreconstructed hard-nosed right-wing cabal.

The Court of American opinion on abortion:

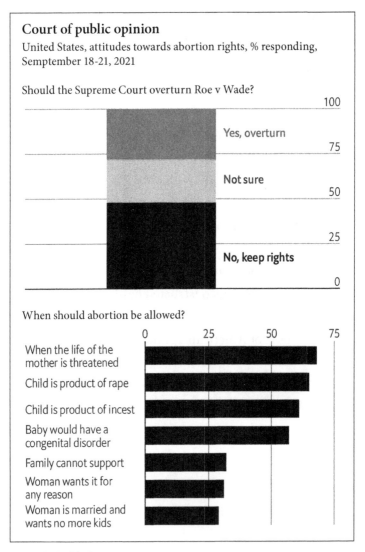

Source: YouGov/The Economist

Furthermore, Biden was not Obama. The GOP had subtly played the race card with him. It stoked fears that millions would lose their health care coverage under

Obamacare, and it would cost taxpayers untold billions in tax hikes and government spending. In 2022 racial paranoia about a Black president and the health care controversy were far removed from the nation's front-burner issues. This potentially could make for a much closer and more fluid midterm election, which held many potential opportunities for the president's party to hold its own in the election.

At the same time, it posed potential obstacles for the GOP to stumble over. That would make the 2022 midterms nothing like the disastrous 2014 midterms for the Democrats—that nearly all predicted.

That was the hope anyway for the Democrats.

Appendix

A Democracy Crisis in the Making
How State Legislatures are Politicizing,
Criminalizing, and Interfering with
Election Administration
2022 Edition
Law Forward, Protect Democracy,
and States United Democracy Center

One year ago, we published A Democracy Crisis in the Making: How State Legislatures are Politicizing, Criminalizing, and Interfering with Election Administration. We warned that state legislatures were considering a range of bills that would increase the risk of election subversion—that is, the risk that the purported outcome of the election does not reflect the choice of the voters. State by state, legislatures had moved to seize power from professional, non-partisan election administrators and to needlessly expose the running of elections to partisan influence and disruption. As we explained in our initial

Report, this trend increases the risk of a crisis in which the outcome of an election could be decided contrary to the will of the people.

Since our first Report, this effort by state legislatures has not receded. In fact, it has accelerated. This year alone, lawmakers have introduced scores of new bills that increase the likelihood of election subversion, whether directly or indirectly. In some cases, the potential subversion is quite direct—for example, bills that give the legislature the power to choose a victor contrary to the voters' will. In others, the impact is less direct but still dangerous. Some bills would introduce dysfunction and chaos into the election system and could lead to delay, uncertainty, and confusion, all of which could provide cover for subversion.

We issued our first Report less than four months after the January 6, 2021, attack on the U.S. Capitol, itself a violent attempt to subvert the voters' choice. In that Report, we identified 148 bills that had been filed that would allow state legislatures to politicize, criminalize, or interfere with elections. Today, at roughly the same point in the calendar year, legislatures in 33 states are considering 229 bills that do the same—175 introduced in this calendar year alone and 54 that rolled over from the last calendar year. A total of 50 bills have been enacted or adopted, 32 last year and 18 thus far this year.

In the first quarter of 2022, significantly more bills have been introduced that would allow legislatures to politicize, criminalize, or interfere with elections than at this time in 2021.

Through the bills discussed in this Report, legislators have attempted to exercise insidious control over practically every step of the electoral process. This includes efforts to shift power to legislatures to directly choose and control election officials and to tie the hands of professional local election administrators. It includes subjecting elections to unprofessional and biased reviews, designed to sow doubt about the legitimacy of results. It includes imposing onerous and unrealistic burdens on election administration—such as a requirement to count all ballots by hand—that will introduce errors and delays, which could be used as a pretext for election subversion. In the most extreme examples, none of which has yet become law, legislators have proposed granting themselves the power to reverse election results altogether and to install their own preferred candidates instead. In many cases, these legislative efforts are as poorly designed as they are misguided, which can make them more dangerous because they are more likely to lead to confusion and chaos.

An Arizona bill, for example, requires election officials to document "voting irregularities"—and attaches a possible criminal penalty for failing to do so—without ever defining the term. In Wisconsin, the speaker of the state Assembly ordered an investigation of the 2020 election, run by a former state Supreme Court justice who has stated that he does not have "a comprehensive understanding or even any understanding of how elections work." In Oklahoma, a bill imagines a 20-person "Election Integrity Committee" to review election results, with no requirement that any of the 20 people have experience in election administration or professional audits.

"In many cases, these legislative efforts are as poorly designed as they are misguided—which can make them more dangerous because they are more likely to lead to confusion and chaos."

Broadly, we classify these legislative maneuvers into five categories:

1. Usurping control over election results. A handful of states have considered bills that would give legislators direct or indirect control over election outcomes, allowing lawmakers to reject the choice of the voters. Although we do not expect any of these proposals to become law in 2022, the fact that they are even being introduced indicates that legislatures are considering the option to overturn future elections. This raises obvious alarms for democracy.

2. Requiring partisan or unprofessional "audits" or reviews. Legislation of this type has surged in 2022. We found 44 bills introduced this year and another five held over from 2021 that propose unprofessional or biased reviews of election results.

They call for procedures that are vague or subject to abuse and in some cases hand the power to call for audits to political parties or the legislature. These bills threaten to call election outcomes perpetually into doubt. They would tie up election administrators and likely would amount to state-sponsored vehicles for disinformation.

3. Seizing power over election responsibilities. Legislatures have proposed shifting power from professional election administrators to partisan legislatures or legislatively appointed officials. These bills increase the danger of partisan election manipulation and raise the risk of an election crisis. We have found 38 bills introduced this year and another 13 held over from 2021 that fall into this category.

4. Creating unworkable burdens in election administration. Legislatures have proposed or passed 93 bills this year and held over 21 from 2021 that increase the risk of subversion by intruding on the granular details of election administration. One particularly dangerous flavor of these bills, under consideration in six states, would require all ballots to be counted by hand, practically guaranteeing delays, higher rates of counting error, and increased risk of tampering by bad actors.

5. Imposing disproportionate criminal or other penalties. Legislatures have proposed to subject election officials to criminal prosecution for poorly defined offenses and have created criminal liability for steps that election officials routinely take to help voters cast ballots. States are also escalating the enforcement of election laws, by creating entirely new law enforcement agencies. We found 54 of these bills introduced so far in 2022 and another 18 held over from 2021 which encourage distrust in elections and election officials and interfere with effective election ad-

ministration. See Chart 2. Left unchecked, these legislative proposals threaten to paralyze the smooth functioning of elections. Election administrators could be left powerless to stop voter intimidation. Election rules could devolve into a confusing and contradictory tangle, subject to change at the whims of partisan lawmakers. Election results could be endlessly called into question and subjected to never-ending, destructive reviews conducted based on no responsible standard. At the extreme, election results could simply be tossed aside and the will of the people ignored.

Source: http://statesuniteddemocracy.org/wp-content/uploads/2022/05/DCITM_2022.pdf

Notes

Introduction

Jason Lemon, "Republicans Put More Stock in 2022 Midterms Than Democrats: Poll," Newsweek, March 24, 2022

www.newsweek.com/republicans-put-more-stock-2022-midterms-democrats-poll-1691619

Stephen Collinson, "McConnell haunts Democrats with new threat to block Biden court nominee," CNN, June 15, 2021

www.cnn.com/2021/06/15/politics/mitch-mcconnell-biden-agenda-manchin/index.html

"Americans in new poll divided on control of Congress," The Hill, January 26, 2022

http://news.yahoo.com/americans-poll-divided-control-congress-180209555.html?fr=sycsrp_catchall

"Americans' Preferences for One-Party Control vs. Divided Control of Government (Trends), Gallup, " nd

http://news.gallup.com/poll/243653/americans-preferences-one-party-control-divided-control-government-trends.aspx

The Trump quote in Burns and Martin, This Will Not Pass, 334

The Biden quote, This Will Not Pass, 408

1
The Tortured History of the Midterms

Don Gonyea, "The Devastating History Of Midterm Elections," NPR, October 30, 2014

www.npr.org/2014/10/30/360133533/the-devastating-history-of-midterm-elections

Terrence P. Jeffrey, "Biggest Midterm House Losses Since WWII: Obama (-63), Truman (-55), Clinton (-54)," CNSNews, November 5, 2018

http://cnsnews.com/news/article/terence-p-jeffrey/obama-63-truman-55-clinton-54-have-biggest-midterm-house-losses-wwii

"United States midterm election," wikipedia, nd

http://en.wikipedia.org/wiki/United_States_midterm_election

Walter Coffey, "The 1862 Federal Elections," Civil War Months,

http://civilwarmonths.com/2017/11/04/the-1862-federal-elections/

Olivia B. Waxman," Why Do Midterm Elections Even Exist? Here's Why the Framers Scheduled Things This Way," Time, November 5, 2018

http://time.com/5443162/why-midterm-elections-exist-history/

Kimberley Amadeo, "The U.S. Senate, What It Does and Its Power," The Balance, December 31, 2021

www.thebalance.com/us-senate-what-it-does-how-it-affects-the-us-economy-3305996

John W, Schoen," Incumbents in Congress are hard to beat—and a lot of it has to do with money," CNBC, April 26, 2018

www.cnbc.com/2018/04/26/here-is-why-incumbents-in-congress-are-hard-to-beat.html

"H.J.Res.5 - Proposing an amendment to the Constitution of the United States to provide for four-year terms for Representatives and to limit the number of terms Senators and Representatives may serve, " congress.gov, nd

www.congress.gov/bill/104th-congress/house-joint-resolution/5

"Congress and the Public," Gallup, nd

http://news.gallup.com/poll/1600/congress-public.aspx

Lydia Saad, "Congress Approval Lowest in 2021 as Democrats Turn Negative," Gallup, October 26, 2021

http://news.gallup.com/poll/356591/congress-approval-lowest-2021-democrats-turn-negative.aspx

"16 Reasons Why Congress Has a Low Approval rating," fourwinds 10.com, March 14, 2013

http://fourwinds10.com/siterun_data/government/fraud/us_government/news.php?q=1363457536

www.law.cornell.edu/supct/html/93-1456.ZO.html \

Robert Longley, "Why No Term Limits for Congress? The Constitution," Thoughtco.com, April 16, 2022

www.thoughtco.com/why-no-term-limits-for-congress-3974547

Joan Biskupic, "Congressional Term Limits Struck Down," Washington Post, May 23, 1995 www.washingtonpost.com/wp-srv/politics/special/termlimits/stories/052395.htm

Lydia Saad, "Americans Call for Term Limits, End to Electoral College," Gallup, January 18, 2013

http://news.gallup.com/poll/159881/americans-call-term-limits-end-electoral-college.aspx

Lyndon B. Johnson, "Annual Message to the Congress on the State of the Union," The American Presidency Project, January 12, 1966

www.presidency.ucsb.edu/documents/annual-message-the-congress-the-state-the-union-27

"Biennial Elections," History, Art & Archives, nd

http://history.house.gov/Institution/Origins-Development/Biennial-Elections/

Ed Kilgore, "No Lindsey Graham, 2022 Won't be another 1994 Landslide," NY Magazine, July 2021

http://nymag.com/intelligencer/2021/07/no-lindsey-graham-2022-wont-be-another-1994-landslide.html

Amber Phillips, "What are the Midterms?" Washington Post, December 14, 2021What

www.msn.com/en-us/news/politics/what-are-the-midterms/ar-AARNvNW

"1838 and 1839 United States House of Representatives election," Wikipedia, nd

http://en.wikipedia.org/wiki/1838_and_1839_United_States_House_of_Representatives_election

Geoffrey Skelley and Kyle Kondick, "How Midterms Do (and Do Not) Differ from Presidential Elections," Center for Politics.org, March 2, 2017

http://centerforpolitics.org/crystalball/articles/how-midterms-do-and-do-not-differ-from-presidential-elections/

2
The President's Party Midterm Swoon

Eric Bradner, " 'They got what they ordered, right?': Democrats search for a midterm message at party gatherings," CNN, March 13, 2022

www.cnn.com/2022/03/12/politics/democrats-midterms-message-2022-biden/index.html

Robert S. Erikson, "The Puzzle of Midterm Loss," The Journal of Politics, Vol. 50, No. 4 (Nov., 1988), pp. 1011-1029

www.jstor.org/stable/2131389

The Biden-Dole meeting in Burns and Martin, "They Will Not Pass," 282

Dylan Matthews, "40 maps and charts that explain the 2014 midterm elections," vox, November 5, 2014

www.vox.com/2014/11/5/7160523/40-maps-and-charts-that-explain-the-2014-midterm-elections

Earl Ofari Hutchinson, "What Trump's Disturbing Race-Baiting Means for His Campaign," highbrowmagazine.com, November 30, 2015

www.highbrowmagazine.com/5465-what-trumps-disturbing-race-baiting-means-his-campaign

"The Global State of Democracy 2021," IDEA International, November 22, 2021

www.idea.int/publications/catalogue/global-state-democracy-2021

The Canadian UN ambassador on the threat to US democracy in Burns and Martin, They Will Not Pass, 430

"2016 U.S. presidential election mapped," vividmaps.com, nd

http://vividmaps.com/2016-us-presidential-election-results/

"US added to list of 'backsliding' democracies for first time," theguardian.com, November 22, 2021

www.theguardian.com/us-news/2021/nov/22/us-list-backsliding-democracies-civil-liberties-international

Elizabeth Colbert, "How Politics got so Polarized," NY Magazine, January 3, 2022

www.newyorker.com/magazine/2022/01/03/how-politics-got-so-polarized

"Losses by the President's Party in Midterm Elections, 1862 – 2014," vitalstats.com, nd

www.brookings.edu/wp-content/uploads/2017/01/vitalstats_ch2_tbl4.pdf

John Bresnahan, "Clinton: Midterms won't be '94 repeat," Politico, September 27, 2009

www.politico.com/story/2009/09/clinton-midterms-wont-be-94-repeat-027647

Alex Henderson, "Are Trump And Gingrich Preparing New 'Contract On America'?," The National Memo, May 23, 2022

www.nationalmemo.com/gingrich-trump-contract-on-america

Earl Ofari Hutchinson, "Why a Shrinking Tea Party Still Holds the Nation Hostage," Huff Post, October 2, 2013

www.huffpost.com/entry/why-a-shrinking-tea-party_b_4026098

Earl Ofari Hutchinson, "Mid-Term Election Danger Signs Loom Big for Democrats," thehutchinsonreport.net, February 14, 2018

www.thehutchinsonreport.net/mid-term-election-danger-signs-loom-big-democrats/

Gabriela Saldivia, "Trump Says Of Midterm Losses, 'My Name Wasn't On The Ballot'," NPR, November 18, 2018

www.npr.org/2018/11/18/669037945/trump-says-of-midterm-losses-my-name-wasn-t-on-the-ballot

Mara Liasson," The Democratic Party Got Crushed During The Obama Presidency. Here's Why," NPR, March 4, 2016

www.npr.org/2016/03/04/469052020/the-democratic-party-got-crushed-during-the-obama-presidency-heres-why

Andrew Prokop," The presidential penalty," vox, March 1, 2022

www.vox.com/22899204/midterm-elections-president-biden-thermostatic-opinion

"2006 Midterm Politics," historylearniingsite.co.uk, nd

www.historylearningsite.co.uk/american-politics/2006-midterm-elections/2006-midterm-results/

"1986 Midterm Elections," conservapedia.com, nd

www.conservapedia.com/1986_Midterm_Elections

Don Gonyea, "The Devastating History Of Midterm Elections," NPR, October 30, 2014

www.npr.org/2014/10/30/360133533/the-devastating-history-of-midterm-elections

Michael Corcoran, "Lessons From the 2006 Midterms: Will Democrats Disappoint Again?," truthout.org, September 16,2016

http://truthout.org/articles/lessons-from-the-2006-midterms-will-democrats-disappoint-again/

The Biden plea to Adams for midterm help is in Burns and Martin, This Will Not Pass, 321

3
The GOP's Midterm Bullseye

This is a sampling of the many headline articles predicting disaster for the Democrats in the 2022 midterms in various mainstream newspapers, magazines, and online in news outlets such as CNN beginning in mid-2021

Biden pushed to campaign for swing state Democrats in Burns and Martin, They Will Not Pass, 421

"Voter Turnout Demographics," electproject.org, nd

www.electproject.org/home/voter-turnout/demographics

"Current Population Survey Voting and Registration Supplement," data.gov, March 11.2021

http://catalog.data.gov/dataset/current-population-survey-voting-and-registration-supplement

The Romney targeting in Burns and Martin, They Will Not Pass, 336

David Frum, "Beto's Loss Was a Blessing in Disguise for Democrats," The Atlantic, November 2018

www.theatlantic.com/ideas/archive/2018/11/why-democrats-won-2018-midterms/575179/

Melissa Herrmann and David Jones, "How Democrats Won the House," CBS News, November 7, 2018

www.cbsnews.com/news/how-democrats-won-the-house-2018-midterm-elections-today-2018-11-06/

Zeke Miller and Darlene Superville, "Trump says Democratic Convention was Gloomiest in History," AP, August 21, 2020

www.wkbn.com/news/national-world/trump-says-democrats-convention-was-gloomiest-in-history/

Meg Wagner, et.al., "House impeaches Trump for role in deadly Capitol riot," CNN, January 13, 2021 www.cnn.com/politics/live-news/house-trump-impeachment-vote-01-13-21/h_3ad9ce3f2eb5b2e89312a6d353996436

Burns, Alexander and Martin, Jonathan, This Will Not Pass: Trump, Biden, and the Battle for America's Future (New York: Simon & Schuster, 2022), 271

Burns, Alexander and Martin, Jonathan, McConnell backing Trump for president in 2024 in Burs and Martin, This Will Not Pass, 349

Harry Enten, "Do Republicans Really Have A Big Turnout Advantage In Midterms?," fivethirtyeight.com, January 9, 2018

http://fivethirtyeight.com/features/do-republicans-really-have-a-big-turnout-advantage-in-midterms/

Julie Herschfeld Davis, "Trump Rallies West Virginia midterms," NY Times, August 21, 2018

www.nytimes.com/2018/08/21/us/politics/trump-rallies-west-virginia-midterms.html

Aaron Mak, "Many Top Donors to "Black Americans for the President's Agenda" Are, in Fact, Wealthy White People," Slate, October 2018

http://slate.com/news-and-politics/2018/10/black-americans-for-the-presidents-agenda-donors-racist-arkansas-ad.html

Lee Moran," NRCC Uses Menacing Message About Trump To Push Republicans Into Repeat Donations," Huff Post, April 8, 2021

www.huffpost.com/entry/nrcc-donald-trump-menacing-message_n_606ebb92c5b6885a6f2c660a

Marty Johnson, "Critical race theory becomes focus of midterms, The Hill, July 22, 2021

http://thehill.com/homenews/house/564218-critical-race-theory-becomes-focus-of-midterms/

Christina Wilkie, "Trump cranks up attacks on the Black Lives Matter movement for racial justice," CNBC, June 25, 2020

www.cnbc.com/2020/06/25/trump-attacks-black-lives-matter-racial-justice-movement.html

4
Culture Wars, Vote Suppression and Messaging

The 2018 down ballot election results in Burns and Martin, They Will Not Pass, 120-122

Trump on the Virginia governor race in Burns and Martin, They Will Not Pass, 434

Tommy Christopher, "DNC Chair Jaime Harrison Rips GOP as Trump Party of Fear and Fraud," Mediaite, January 22, 2022DNC Chair Jaime

www.msn.com/en-us/news/politics/dnc-chair-jaime-harrison-rips-gop-as-trump-party-of-fear-fascism-and-fraud/ar-AAT2MI4

David Jackson, "Anti-Trans Bills, Midterms," USA Today, May 4, 2022

www.usatoday.com/story/news/politics/2022/05/04/republicans-anti-transgender-bills-midterm/7384097001/?gnt-cfr=1

Neil Munro, "Senate Republicans Promise to Oppose Elite-Backed Transgender Ideology,"Breitbart, February 2, 2022

www.breitbart.com/health/2022/02/22/senate-republicans-promise-oppose-elite-backed-transgender-ideology/

Neil Munro, "Poll Shows Transgender Ideology Losing Support," Breibart, November 8, 2011

www.breitbart.com/health/2021/11/08/poll-shows-transgender-ideology-losing-support/

Earl Ofari Hutchinson, "Doing Everything Under the Sun to Make the Blue Wave a Trickle," thehutchinsonreport.net, October 21, 2018 www.thehutchinsonreport.net/doing-everything-under-the-sun-to-make-the-blue-wave-a-trickle/

Earl Ofari Hutchinson, " How Trump Plans to Win and Its Scary," thehutchinsonreport.net, August 23, 2020

www.thehutchinsonreport.net/how-trump-plans-to-win-and-its-scary/

Elliot Ramos, "Nearly 240 Anti-LGBTQ Bills Filed in 2022," NBC News, March 20. 2022Nearly 240 anti-LGBTQ bills filed in

www.nbcnews.com/nbc-out/out-politics-and-policy/nearly-240-anti-lgbtq-bills-filed-2022-far-targeting-trans-people-rcna20418

Joseph Ax, "Republican-Backed Bills Restricting Vote Advance Across U.S., Report Finds," US News, May 28, 2021

www.usnews.com/news/top-news/articles/2021-05-28/republican-backed-bills-restricting-vote-advance-across-us-report-finds

Earl Ofari Hutchinson, "GOP voter suppression poses grave danger to Democrats in 2020," Bay State Banner, November 29, 2018

www.baystatebanner.com/2018/11/29/gop-voter-suppression-poses-grave-danger-to-democrats-in-2020/

Biden's voting rights bill dilemma in Burns and Martin, They Will Not Pass, 322

Matt Lavietes, "Anti-LGBTQ school bills go national as 19 other states consider Florida-style laws, NBC News, April 11, 2022

www.aol.com/floridas-not-alone-19-other-133051643.html

Harry Enten, "Off-the-charts gas price hikes are a big problem for Democrats," CNN, June 4, 2022

www.cnn.com/2022/06/04/politics/gas-prices-democrats-election-2022/index.html

"1978 US Elections"

http://en.wikipedia.org/wiki/1978_United_States_elections

Spencer Brown, "CBS Poll Shows How Badly Biden Is Losing the Messaging War, "Townhall, April 11. 2022

http://townhall.com/tipsheet/spencerbrown/2022/04/11/cbs-poll-shows-how-badly-biden-is-losing-the-messaging-war-n2605738

D. Hunter Schwarz, "How Republicans plan to beat 'Biden Democrats' and take back Congress," Deseret News, August 26, 2021 www.deseret.com/2021/8/26/22631095/how-republicans-hope-to-beat-biden-democrats-and-take-back-congress-2022-election-covid-afghanistan

Anzalone memo to Biden in Burns and Martin, This Will Not Pass, 320

Geoffrey James, "Why Republicans sell Better than Democrats, "CBS News, December 10, 2010

www.cbsnews.com/news/why-republicans-sell-better-than-democrats/

Kimberley Atkins Stahr, "The Democrats' messaging problem, and how to fix it," WBUR, January 1. 2022

www.wbur.org/onpoint/2022/01/21/biden-democrat-problem-republican-messaging-politics

Brett Samuels, "Biden hits 63 percent approval rating in new AP poll, "The Hill"

http://thehill.com/homenews/administration/552596-biden-hits-63-percent-approval-rating-in-new-ap-poll/

Andrew Mark Miller, "Biden approval rating plummets to 39%, down 24 points from last year: AP poll, Fox News, May 20, 2022

www.foxnews.com/politics/biden-approval-rating-plummets-down-24-points-last-year

5
The Disappearing Voter

Jeff Zeleney, "Biden authorizes $15 million transfer from DNC to House and Senate campaign committees," CNN, February 3, 2022

www.cnn.com/2022/02/03/politics/cash-transfer-biden-dnc-house-senate-midterms/index.html

Jonathan Martin, "Young Black Voices Skepticism on Hillary Clinton Worrying Democrats," NY Times, September 5, 2016

www.nytimes.com/2016/09/05/us/politics/young-blacks-voice-skepticism-on-hillary-clinton-worrying-democrats.html

Jacob Fabina. "Despite Pandemic Challenges, 2020 Election Had Largest Increase in Voting Between Presidential Elections on Record," US Census Bureau, April 29, 2021

www.census.gov/library/stories/2021/04/record-high-turnout-in-2020-general-election.html

Asma Khalid, et.al, "On The Sidelines Of Democracy: Exploring Why So Many Americans Don't Vote," NPR, September 10, 2018

www.npr.org/2018/09/10/645223716/on-the-sidelines-of-democracy-exploring-why-so-many-americans-dont-vote

Richard Harris, "How will turnout compare to last time? Four states already have more votes than they did in 2016," NY Times, November 3, 2020

www.nytimes.com/2020/11/03/us/politics/election-2016-voter-comparison.html

Madison Hall. "How the 2020 election results compare to 2016, in 9 maps and charts," Business Insider, November 18, 2020

www.businessinsider.com/2016-2020-electoral-maps-exit-polls-compared-2020-11#predictably-partisan-voters-cast-their-ballots-along-party-lines-but-many-more-moderate-voters-chose-biden-over-trump-in-2020-helping-to-propel-the-democratic-nominee-to-victory-9

Gustavo Lopez," Dislike of candidates or campaign issues was most common reason for not voting in 2016," Pew Research Center, June 1, 2017

www.pewresearch.org/fact-tank/2017/06/01/dislike-of-candidates-or-campaign-issues-was-most-common-reason-for-not-voting-in-2016/

Daniel Weeks, "Why Are the Poor and Minorities Less Likely to Vote?," The Atlantic, April 1, 2014

www.theatlantic.com/politics/archive/2014/01/why-are-the-poor-and-minorities-less-likely-to-vote/282896/

Sam Fulwood III, "Why Young, Minority, and Low-Income Citizens Don't Vote, "CAP, November 6, 2014

www.americanprogress.org/article/why-young-minority-and-low-income-citizens-dont-vote/

Alex Ura, et.al.," Polling places for urban voters of color would be cut under Texas Senate's version of voting bill being negotiated with House," The Texas Tribune, May 23, 2021

www.texastribune.org/2021/05/23/texas-voting-polling-restrictions/

Sarina Vij, "Why Minority Voters Have a Lower Voter Turnout," American Bar Assn., June 25,2020

www.americanbar.org/groups/crsj/publications/human_rights_magazine_home/voting-in-2020/why-minority-voters-have-a-lower-voter-turnout/

"Top States for Latino Voters," Pew Research Center, nd

www.pewresearch.org/wp-content/uploads/2020/01/ft_2020.01.31_latinovoters_02.png?resize=640,382

Hannah Griffin, "Keep it Clean? How Negative Keep it Clean? How Negative Campaigns Affect Campaigns Affect Voter Turnout," Res Publica, July12, 2012

http://digitalcommons.iwu.edu/cgi/viewcontent.cgi?article=1193&context=respublica

Mike Bebernes, "Why so many Americans don't vote, Yahoo News, March 13, 2020

http://news.yahoo.com/why-so-many-americans-dont-vote-141725897.html?fr=sycsrp_catchall

Earl Ofari Hutchinson, "The Brutal Truth: The Felon Voting Ban is a Black Ban, IBW, November 6, 2018

http://ibw21.org/editors-choice/brutal-truth-felon-voting-ban-black-ban/

www.bloomberg.com/news/articles/2018-11-06/why-americans-don-t-vote-in-the-midterm-election

George Packer," Poor, White and Republican, "The Atlantic, February 13, 2012

www.newyorker.com/news/daily-comment/poor-white-and-republican

BC Editorial Team, "Why is the Poor Community of America Willing to Vote Republican," Bay Citizen, May 10, 2010

www.baycitizen.org/why-is-the-poor-community-of-america-willing-to-vote-republican/

"Joe Biden on Voting Rights for Felons," Democratic Underground, April 29, 2019"

www.democraticunderground.com/128797988

6
Breaking the Democrat's Mid Term Jinx

Ali Zaslav, "McConnell: 2022 midterms 'will be about the future, not about the past," CNN, November 8, 2021

www.cnn.com/2021/11/08/politics/mitch-mcconnell-2022-comments/index.html

Kate Sullivan, "Biden wades into the midterms by endorsing Oregon Democratic congressman facing progressive challenger," CNN, April 25, 2022

www.cnn.com/2022/04/25/politics/biden-2022-endorsement-schrader-oregon/index.html

Ed Kilgore, "Republicans can still fumble away the Senate," New York Magazine, April 27, 2022

http://nymag.com/intelligencer/article/republicans-can-still-fumble-away-the-senate.html

Jeff Greenfeld, "Opinion | History Shows the Democrats' Midterm Doom Isn't Preordained," Politico, April 7, 2022

www.politico.com/news/magazine/2022/04/07/history-democrats-midterms-disaster-biden-trouble-00023175

GOP opposition to January 6 Capitol riot commission in Burns and Martin, They Will Not Pass, 364

Tom Boggioni, "Donald Trump calls January 6th 'the greatest movement in the history of our Country' ahead of hearings," Alternet, January 9, 2022

www.alternet.org/2022/06/donald-trump-calls-january-6th/

Olivia Beavers, et.al. "House GOP's new midterm headache: Candidates tied to the Capitol riot," Politico, August 4, 2021

www.politico.com/news/2021/08/04/capitol-riot-house-gop-midterm-502461

"The Economist/YouGov Poll," The Economist, June 13-15, 2021

http://docs.cdn.yougov.com/1oyiu6tamw/econTabReport.pdf

Sarah Ferris, "House Dem campaign chief warns the majority at risk without message reboot," Politico, August 3, 2021

www.politico.com/news/2021/08/03/sean-patrick-maloney-democrats-house-majority-502265

Nicholas Hensley, "Democrats Learned Nothing from 2016 Loss," reformparty.org, May 6, 2017

http://reformparty.org/democrats-learned-nothing-2016-loss/

Paul Steinhauser, "RNC spotlights 'massive investments' in data, ground game, to grow GOP ahead of November's midterms," Fox News, February 23, 2022

www.foxbusiness.com/politics/rnc-investments-data-ground-game-november-midterms

Chuck Todd, et.al., "Democrats face Double Digit Enthusiasm Deficit Ahead of Midterms." NBC News, January 24, 2022Democrats face double-digit

www.nbcnews.com/politics/meet-the-press/democrats-face-double-digit-enthusiasm-deficit-ahead-midterms-n1287910

Harry Enten, "Why polls may be underestimating Republicans," CNN, February 19, 2022

www.cnn.com/2022/02/19/politics/enthusiasm-republican-midterms-high/index.html

"Mark Murray, "Divisive Voters Sour on nation's Direction," NBC News, January 23, 2022

www.nbcnews.com/politics/meet-the-press/downhill-divisive-americans-sour-nation-s-direction-new-nbc-news-n1287888

Luca Cacciotore, "Obama on Midterms: Dems Have 'Got a Story to Tell, Just Got to Tell It'," Newsmax,May 23, 2022 www.newsmax.com/politics/obama-midterms-2022-election-red-wave/2022/04/05/id/1064468/

Nicholas Riccardi, "Biden's approval dips to lowest of presidency: AP-NORC poll, AP News, May 20,2022

http://apnews.com/article/biden-approval-rating-drops-ap-norc-poll-d41bce85e1b062b588a32908b2affa65

http://apnews.com/article/ap-norc-poll-inflation-economy-38b6b4953a09d12164cd92ff49a8d758

Melissa Herrmann, "How Democrats won the House," CBS News, November 6, 2018

www.cbsnews.com/news/how-democrats-won-the-house-2018-midterm-elections-today-2018-11-06/

Harry Enten, "Americans are more worried about crime than at any time this century," CNN, June 8, 2022

www.msn.com/en-us/news/politics/americans-are-more-worried-about-crime-than-at-any-other-time-this-century/ar-AAYf1TT

7
Warring on Voting Rights

Peter Zampa, "Voting rights in the spotlight as 2022 midterms approach," NBC 12, December 31, 2021 www.nbc12.com/2021/12/30/voting-rights-spotlight-2022-midterms-approach/

Ariane deVouge, et.al.," Supreme Court says Arizona limits don't violate Voting Rights Act. CNN, July 1, 2021

www.cnn.com/2021/07/01/politics/voting-rights-act-supreme-court-ruling/index.html

"New Polling: Voting Behavior and The Impact of The Black Vote in 2018 Midterm Elections," America's Voice, November 19, 2016

http://americasvoice.org/press_releases/new-polling-voting-behavior-and-the-impact-of-the-black-vote-in-2018-midterm-elections/

William Yeomans," GOP war on Voting Rights Act," Politico, September 11, 2012

www.politico.com/story/2012/09/the-gop-war-on-the-voting-rights-act-081050

"A History of the Voting Rights Act," ACLU, nd

www.aclu.org/issues/voting-rights/voting-rights-act/history-voting-rights-act

Ari Berman, "The GOP's Attack on Voting Rights Was the Most Under-Covered Story of 2016, The Nation, November 9, 2016 www.thenation.com/article/archive/the-gops-attack-on-voting-rights-was-the-most-under-covered-story-of-2016/

Herb Denton, "Reagan signs Voter Rights extension, " Washington Post , June 30, 1982

www.washingtonpost.com/archive/politics/1982/06/30/reagan-signs-voting-rights-act-extension/b59370f1-fc93-4e2f-b417-2b614ea55910/

Ian Millhiser, "Chief Justice Roberts's lifelong crusade against voting rights, explained," Vox, September 18, 2020

www.msn.com/en-us/news/politics/chief-justice-roberts-s-lifelong-crusade-against-voting-rights-explained/ar-BB19aW31

The Heritage Foundation, "The Facts About H.R. 1: The "For the People Act of 2021"

www.heritage.org/election-integrity/report/the-facts-about-hr-1-the-the-people-act-2021

Congresss.gov, "H.R.1 - For the People Act of 2019,"congressgov.com, nd

www.congress.gov/bill/116th-congress/house-bill/1/text#toc-H67D4FBDA0E0747BE8E6548AA184D330F

"An Assessment of MINORITY VOTING RIGHTS ACCESS in the United States," US Govt. Publications, nd www.usccr.gov/files/pubs/2018/Minority_Voting_Access_2018.pdf

8
Destroying Two Presidents

"Biden roasts Trump, GOP, himself at correspondents' dinner," CNBC, May 1, 2022

www.cnbc.com/2022/05/01/biden-roasts-trump-gop-himself-at-correspondents-dinner.html

Glenn Kessler, "When did McConnell say he wanted to make Obama a 'one-term president'?, Washington Post, September 25, 2012

www.washingtonpost.com/blogs/fact-checker/post/when-did-mcconnell-say-he-wanted-to-make-obama-a-one-term-president/2012/09/24/79fd5cd8-0696-11e2-afff-d6c-7f20a83bf_blog.html

Mike Allen, "McConnell sees Dem 'queasiness' on budget," Politico, March 24, 2009

www.politico.com/story/2009/03/mcconnell-sees-dem-queasiness-on-budget-020439

Hannah Blaeu," Poll: More Voters Say Republicans Better than Democrats at Handling Key Economic Issues," Breibart, April 30, 2022 www.breitbart.com/politics/2022/04/30/poll-more-voters-say-republicans-better-than-democrats-at-handling-key-economic-issues/

Veronique deRugy," Debt and Deficit under Obama Administration," Mercatus Center, December 8, 2016

www.mercatus.org/publications/government-spending/debt-and-deficit-under-obama-administration

Napp Nazworth, "Poll: Unemployment Is Most Important Problem; Obama's Jobs Bill Favored," The Christian Post, September 15, 2011

www.christianpost.com/news/poll-unemployment-is-most-important-problem-obamas-jobs-bill-favored.html

Julia Manchester, "Democrats look to shake off 'defund the police', The Hill, February 6, 2022

http://thehill.com/homenews/campaign/592920-democrats-look-to-shake-off-defund-the-police-as-crime-rises/

Kendall Karson, "64% of Americans oppose 'defund the police' movement, key goals: POLL," ABC News, June 12, 2020

http://abcnews.go.com/Politics/64-americans-oppose-defund-police-movement-key-goals/story?id=71202300

Maeve Reston, "California voters send a stark message to Democrats on crime and homelessness," CNN, June 7, 2022 www.cnn.com/2022/06/07/politics/primary-elections-june-7-california-iowa/index.html

Kate Sullivan, Biden says Tuesdays Primaries show voters want harder stance on crime and gun violence, CNN, June 8, 2022

www.msn.com/en-us/news/politics/biden-says-tuesdays-primary-results-show-voters-want-harder-stance-on-crime-and-gun-violence/ar-AAYeGJ5

Jeremy B. White, San Francisco district attorney ousted in recall election," Politico, June 8, 2022

www.politico.com/news/2022/06/08/chesa-boudin-san-francisco-district-attorney-recall-00038002

David Wright, "Republicans hammer Democrats on inflation in midterms advertising, CNN, March 18, 2022

www.abc12.com/news/politics/republicans-hammer-democrats-on-inflation-in-midterms-advertising/article_0d6a2690-9ce0-5659-998d-2997d98d0a55.html

Gary Langer, "Economic discontent, criticisms of Biden lift GOP to record early advantage: POLL, ABC News, November 13, 2021

http://abcnews.go.com/Politics/economic-discontent-criticisms-biden-lift-gop-record-early/story?id=81095146

Harry Enten, "More bad news for Biden: More Americans are blaming him for the state of the economy," CNN, May 5, 2022

www.cnn.com/2022/05/05/politics/biden-economy-midterms-poll-blame/index.html

Amber Phillips, "Biden's Budget and the Midterms," Washington Post, March 28, 2022

www.washingtonpost.com/politics/2022/03/28/biden-budget-democrat-midterms/

Li Zhou, "What Biden is really saying in his new budget," vox, March 28, 2022

www.vox.com/23000382/joe-biden-budget-police

"Fact Sheet: President Biden's Budget Invests in Reducing Gun Crime to Make Our Communities Safer," The White House, March 28, 2022

www.whitehouse.gov/omb/briefing-room/2022/03/28/fact-sheet-president-bidens-budget-invests-in-reducing-gun-crime-to-make-our-communities-safer/

Dan Roberts, " McConnell warns Obama not to 'poison the well' after midterms rout," The Guardian, November 5, 2014

www.theguardian.com/us-news/2014/nov/05/mcconnell-warns-obama-poison-the-well-midterms

Schumer warning to Biden about McConnell in Burns and Martin, This Will Not Pass, 260

Tommy Christopher," New Poll: Overturning Roe More Likely to Help Democrats Than Republicans—By Double," Mediaite, May 7, 2022

www.mediaite.com/news/new-poll-overturning-roe-more-likely-to-help-democrats-than-republicans-by-double/

Tristan Smith, "President Biden says Roe v. Wade should be upheld and his office supports 'a woman's right to choose', in wake of leaked Supreme Court documents," masslive.com, May 3, 2022

www.masslive.com/news/2022/05/president-biden-says-roe-v-wade-should-be-upheld-and-his-office-supports-a-womans-right-to-choose-in-wake-of-leaked-supreme-court-documents.html

Conclusion
Midterm Lessons

Lawrence Friedman," McConnell's unconstitutional blockade of Garland poisoned subsequent proceedings, The Hill, February 16, 2022

http://thehill.com/opinion/judiciary/594574-mcconnells-unconstitutional-blockade-of-garland-poisoned-subsequent/

Adam Brewster, "A test for Trump as Michigan GOP gathers," Yahoo News, April 22, 2022

http://news.yahoo.com/test-trump-michigan-gop-gathers-203221631.html?fr=sycsrp_catchall

Caitlin Dickson, "Poll: Two-thirds of Republicans still think the 2020 election was rigged," Yahoo News, August 4, 2021

http://news.yahoo.com/poll-two-thirds-of-republicans-still-think-the-2020-election-was-rigged-165934695.html?fr=sycsrp_catchall

Nick Bunker, "A post-war history of U.S. economic growth," equitablegrowth.org, July 30, 2014

http://equitablegrowth.org/post-war-history-u-s-economic-growth/

Paul Steinhauser, "6 factors that will influence the midterms, CNN, May 2, 2014

http://edition.cnn.com/2014/05/02/politics/six-factors-midterms/index.htm

Devin Dwyer, "Non-Voters: Younger, Single, Low Paid... Democrats?, ABC News, October 7, 2010

http://abcnews.go.com/Politics/vote-2010-election-voters-outnumber-voters-midterms-pew/story?id=11985301

"Voter Turnout Increased Sharply Across all racial and Ethnic Lines, 2018", courthousenewws.com, May 2019

www.courthousenews.com/wp-content/uploads/2019/05/voter-turnout.png

"Citizens United: The Supreme Court Ruling," Public Citizen, nd

www.citizen.org/article/the-supreme-court-ruling/

Earl Ofari Hutchinson, "A Republican Midterm Wave Will Further Sink Black America," Huff Post, October 31, 2014

www.huffpost.com/entry/a-republican-midterm-wave_b_6083902

Sara Fischer, "Obama: 'I've got to take responsibility' for Democratic loss in midterms," CNN, November 9, 2014

www.cnn.com/2014/11/09/politics/obama-responsibility-midterms/index.html

Postscript

Chris Cilliza, "Why Republicans feel so good about the 2014 midterms, in 1 chart," Washington Post, April 14, 2014

www.washingtonpost.com/news/the-fix/wp/2014/04/14/why-republicans-feel-so-good-about-the-2014-midterms-in-1-chart/

Jon Terbush, "How the Tea Party lost the 2014 midterms, The Week, January 8, 2015

http://theweek.com/articles/442449/how-tea-party-lost-2014-midterms

Susan Davis, "2014 midterm races to test Tea Party power to last, " USA Today, February 23, 2013

www.usatoday.com/story/news/politics/2014/02/23/tea-party-establishment-races-2014/5653423/

Gary Langer, "Midterm Elections 2014: National Exit Poll Reveals Major Voter Discontent," ABC News, November 4, 2014

http://abcnews.go.com/Politics/national-exit-poll-reveals-major-voter-discontent-midterm/story?id=26688877

Ryan Bhandari," Midterm Elections 2014: Key Political Issues to Watch, equities, November 3, 2014

www.equities.com/news/midterm-elections-2014-key-political-issues-to-watch

Harry Enten, "Special Coverage: The 2014 Midterms," fivethirtyeight.com, November 5, 2014

http://fivethirtyeight.com/live-blog/special-coverage-the-2014-midterms/

Mark Moore, "Economy and abortion top voter issues ahead of midterms, 4 in 5 say US on wrong track: poll," NY Post, May 12, 2022

http://nypost.com/2022/05/12/economy-and-abortion-top-voter-issues-before-midterms-poll/

"A clear majority of Americans favour abortion rights," The Economist, September 23, 2021

www.economist.com/graphic-detail/2021/09/23/a-clear-majority-of-americans-favour-abortion-rights

Bibliography

Alexander, Michelle, *The New Jim Crow: Mass Incarceration in the Age of Colorblindness* (New York: New Press, 2020)

Allen Jonathan and Parnes Amy, *Lucky: How Joe Biden Barely Won the Presidency* (New York: Crown, 2021)

Anderson, Carol, *One Person, No Vote: How Voter Suppression Is Destroying Our Democracy* (New York: Bloomsbury Publishing, 2019)

Anderson, Carol, *White Rage: The Unspoken Truth of Our Racial Divide,* 2017

Ansolabehere, Stephen, *Going Negative,* (New York: Free Press, 1997)

Beland, Daniel, *Obamacare Wars: Federalism, State Politics, and the Affordable Care Act* (Studies in Government and Public Policy) (Topeka: University of Kansas Press, 2010)

Bell, Richard C., *Voting: The Ultimate Act of Resistance: The Real Truth from the Voting Rights Battlefields* (New York: Word Assn. Publishers, 2020)

Berman, Ari, *Give Us the Ballot: The Modern Struggle for Voting Rights in America* (New York: Picador, 2016)

Broadwater, Jeff, *Jefferson, Madison, and the Making of the Constitution* (Chapel Hill: University of North Carolina Press, 2019)

Burns, Alexander and Martin, Jonathan, *This Will Not Pass: Trump, Biden and the Battle for America's Future* (New York: Simon & Schuster, 2022)

Clinton, Hillary Rodham, *What Happened* (New York: Simon & Schuster, 2017)

Continetti, Matthew, *The Right: The Hundred-Year War for American Conservatism* (New York: Basic Books, 2022)

Devine, Tim, *Days Of Trump: The Definitive Chronology of the 45th President of the United States* (New York: Battle Press, 2021)

Djonis, Christos, *It's the Economy, Stupid* (Page Publishing, 2018)

Dodd, Lawrence C., *Congress Reconsidered* (New York: CQ Press, 2016)

Genovese, Michael A., *Polls and Politics: The Dilemmas of Democracy* (Binghamton NY: SUNY Press, 2004

Gest, Ted, *Crime & Politics: Big Government's Erratic Campaign for Law and Order* (New York: Oxford University Press, 2003)

Greenburg, Jan Crawford, *Supreme Conflict: The Inside Story of the Struggle for Control of the United States Supreme Court* (New York: Penguin Books, 2008)

Hamilton, Alexander and Madison, James, T*he Federalist Papers* (Dover Thrift Editions: American History) (New York: Dover Publications, 2014)

Hessan, Diane, *Our Common Ground: Insights from Four Years of Listening to American Voters* (Real Clear Publishing, 2021)

Isaac-Dovere, Edward, *Battle for the Soul: Inside the Democrats' Campaigns to Defeat Trump* (New York: Viking, 2021)

Jones, Charles O., *Every Second Year: Congressional Behavior and the Two-Year Term* (Washington, D.C.: The Brookings Institution, 1967).

Jones, David R., *Americans, Congress, and Democratic Responsiveness: Public Evaluations of Congress and Electoral Consequences* (Ann Arbor: University of Michigan Press, 2010)

Kilgore, Ed, *Election 2014: Why the Republicans Swept the Midterms* (College Park: University of Pennsylvania Press, 2015)

Klein, Ezra, *Why We're Polarized* (New York: Simon & Schuster, 2021)

Klinkner, Phillip et.al. *Midterm: The Elections Of 1994 In Context* (Transforming American Politics) (Boulder: Westview Press, 1996)

McGough, Michael, *A Field Guide to the Culture Wars: The Battle over Values from the Campaign Trail to the Classroom* (Religion, Politics, and Public Life) (New York: Praeger, 2008)

McConnell, Mitch, *The Long Game: A Memoir* (New York: Penguin, 2014)

Mann, Thomas E., *It's Even Worse Than It Looks: How the American Constitutional System Collided with the New Politics of Extremism* (New York: Basic Books, 2016)

Marini, John A., *The Politics of Budget Control: Congress, The Presidency and Growth of the Administrative State* (New York: Taylor & Francis, 1992)

Meacham, Jon, *The Soul of America: The Battle for Our Better Angels* (New York: Random House, 2019)

Obama, Barack, *A Promised Land* (New York: Crown 2020)

Ornstein, Norman, *The Broken Branch: How Congress Is Failing America and How to Get It Back on Track* (Institutions of American Democracy Series) (New York: Oxford University Press, 2006}

Rankin, Loren, *Bodies on the Line: At the Front Lines of the Fight to Protect Abortion in America* (Counterpoint, 2022)

Raskin, Jaime, *Unthinkable: Trauma, Truth, and the Trials of American Democracy* (New York: Harper, 2022)

Roth, Zachary, *The Great Suppression: Voting Rights, Corporate Cash, and the Conservative Assault on Democracy* (New York: Crown, 2016)

Sabato, Larry, *Midterm Madness: The Elections of 2002* (Center for Politics Series) (Rowman & Littlefield, 2003)

Sabato, Larry, *The Blue Wave: The 2018 Midterms and What They Mean for the 2020 Elections* (New York: Rowman & Littlefield, 2019)

Sabato, Larry, *Trumped: The 2016 Election That Broke All the Rules* (Rowman & Littlefield, 2017)

Saletan, William, *Bearing Right: How Conservatives Won the Abortion War* (Berkeley: University of California Press, 2004)

Schenker, Jason, *Midterm Economics: The Impact of Midterm Elections on Financial Markets and the Economy* (Prestige Professional Publishing Co., 2018)

Senate Select Committee to Investigate the January 6th Attack on the U.S. Capitol, *The January 6th Report* (Washington DC: Celadon Books, 2022)

Shapiro, Ilya, *Supreme Disorder: Judicial Nominations and the Politics of America's Highest Court* (New York: Regnery Gateway, 2020)

Shapiro, Ira, T*he Betrayal: How Mitch McConnell and the Senate Republicans Abandoned America* (New York: Rowman & Littlefield, 2022)

Shapiro, Ira, *Broken: Can the Senate Save Itself and the Country?* (New York: Rowman & Littlefield, 2018)

Stewart, David O., *The Summer of 1787: The Men Who Invented the Constitution* (New York: Simon & Schuster, 2008)

Theiss-Morse, Elizabeth, et.al., *Political Behavior in Midterm Elections 1st Edition* (New York: CQ Press, 2015)

Woodward, Bob, *Rage* (New York: Simon & Schuster, 2020)

Will, George, *Restoration: Congress, Term Limits and the Recovery of Deliberative Democracy* (New York: Free Press, 1993)

Wonning, Paul, *A Short History of United States Politics - Book 1: The Parties, Presidents and Campaigns* (Mossy Feet Books, 2021)

Zelizer, Julian, *Burning Down the House: Newt Gingrich and the Rise of the New Republican Party* (New York: Penguin, 2021)

Zelizer, Julian, *On Capitol Hill: The Struggles to Reform Congress and Its Consequences, 1948-2000 1st Edition* (New York: Cambridge University Press, 2004)

Index

Abortion, 203-204

Adams, Eric, 54

Affordable Care Act, 80, 129, 192, 193

African American voters, 43, 90-91, 98, 103, 122, 125, 153
 191, 195, 198
    Lover voter turnout, 5, 92
    Support Republicans, 32
    Jim Crow voter exclusion, 146

Arizona low district turnout, 101-103

Asian voters, 156

Biden, Joe, 1, 4, 6, 31, 54, 56, 80, 115, 120, 131, 133, 188,
 192, 197
    American Rescue Plan, 105, 113
    Budget proposal 2022-2023, 168-169, 173-174
    Low approval ratings, 50, 158-159
    Messaging, 81-86
    Trump attacks, 68, 80

Black Americans for Trump, 64
Black Lives Matter, 69, 179
Brown, Kentanji, 73, 175
Bush, George Jr., 2, 33, 52, 46, 104
    Voting Rights Act controversy, 140
Bush, George, Sr., 194
Campaign financing, 195
Carter, Jimmy, 81
Census Bureau Population Survey, 57
Citizens United ruling, 195
Clinton, Bill, 25, 30, 37, 38, 46, 50
Clinton, Hillary, 123, 195
COVID, 29, 66, 176
Congress, 5, 11, 14, 16-17, 18, 22, 56
    Party controls, 4
Congressional Black Caucus, 79
Crime issue impact, 135-136, 179-180
Criminal justice reform, 179
Critical race theory, 116-117
Democrats, 4, 28-29, 54
    Suffer major midterm losses, 29-30, 39-40, 87
    2018 midterm win, 63, 131-132, 133
    2022 midterms, 154, 156, 171, 189
    2022 slender congressional control, 182-183
2022 campaign strategy, 86, 118, 120
Slim control Congress, 182
Democratic National Committee, 1, 2, 86-87, 121, 125, 169, 201

Democratic Congressional Campaign Committee, 86, 118, 120
Dole, Robert, 31-32, 47
Economy importance, 48, 134, 170-171, 187
1862 midterms, 7-8
Eisenhower, Dwight D., 38, 47, 51
Emanuel, Rahm, 53
Inflation fears, 170-171, 188
Felon voting ban, 105-108
Founding Fathers, 12-13, 14
    Constitutional Convention, 15
Garland, Merrick, 87, 182
Gingrich, Newt, 25
    Checks and balances, 11
    Low approval, 16-18
Graham, Lindsey, 4
    "Contract with America," 39
Harris, Kamala, 28
Hispanic voters, 91, 98, 103, 122, 125, 153, 195, 198
House of Representatives, 4, 56, 115
    Midterm changes, 16
    Term limit debate, 19, 21-23
Holder, Eric, 143, 153
January 6 Capitol riot, 34, 58, 117, 118, 184
Johnson, Lyndon Baines, 14-15, 18
Kavanaugh, Brett, 63
Kennedy, John F., 2
Kerry, John, 104

Lincoln, Abraham, 7-8
Madison, James, 20
    Federalist Papers, 20
Minimum wage, 193
McCarthy, Kevin, 117
McConnell, Mitch, 3, 114, 182, 185, 194
    January 6 Capitol riot, 60
    Obama attack, 159-162, 163-165, 193-194
    2022 midterms, 175
    Voting Rights Act, 138
    Block Biden, 175-176
Midterms
    President's party losses, 1-2, 28
    Importance, 1-4
    Gains and losses for parties, 9-10, 35-36, 115, 119, 129
History of midterms, 10-11
    Low voter turnout, 24-25, 59-60
    Swing state crucial, 58
    President's approval ratings importance, 46-47, 49-50, 136
    Midterm voter preferences, 173
Mondale, Walter, 52
New Deal, 2-3, 52
Nixon, Richard, 2, 33, 47
    Southern Strategy, 51
    Watergate, 47, 142, 145
NAACP Voter Survey, 154-155
Native American voters, 101, 102

1994 Midterms, 37-38
Non-voters,
> Identified, 92, 108
> Low fact factors, 97-98
> Minorities, youth, 92
> Negative campaigning, 103-104
> Whites, 94

Obama, Barack, 3, 30, 35, 39, 40, 41, 43, 50, 121, 126, 129
> Obamacare, 17

Midterm record losses, 39, 79

Black vote, 90-92

Downplays poverty, 163
> GOP block initiatives, 174-175, 192, 195, 202

Pelosi, Nancy, 69, 79, 87, 189

Polls, 4, 189
> Whites bias found, 34
> Gender bias, 75
> GOP voter enthusiasm gap, 130
> Low voter turnout advantage, 99
> Critical race theory view, 116-117
> 2018 exit poll, 131-132

Poverty issue, 92-93

Reagan, Ronald, 47, 52-53, 138, 157
> Voting Rights Act, 141

Republicans, 1, 2, 4, 27, 33-34, 55
> Blue collar base, 35, 40, 156, 195
> GOP voter enthusiasm, 2022 midterms, 60-61, 62, 127-129

    Blue collar support, 69-70
    Older white voter edge, 33-34
GOP gains, 36-37
GOP strategy, 66-67
Opposition to LGBT rights, 73-74, 76
Wedge issues, 73-74
Vote suppression, 75-80
Medicaid attacks, 109-110
        Opposes VRA, 135
        Law and order emphasis, 166-167
        State legislature control, 189-196
Republican National Committee, 120, 124-125, 169, 201
Roberts, John, 141, 150
        Memo on Voting Rights Act, 142-143
        Opposition to VRA, 146-147
Romney, Mitt, 59
Roosevelt, Franklin Delano, 2, 32, 52
Russia-Ukraine war, 171
Sanders, Bernie, 123
Scalia, Antonin, 146
Schumer, Chuck, 176
Scott, Rick, 75-76
Senate, 13, 56, 115
        Structure Constitutional Convention, 13
Smith, William French, 141
Stephens, John Paul, 21
Tea Party, 41, 199-201, 202
Thomas, Clarence, 20-21

Transgender attack, 74-75
Truman, Harry, 31
Trump, Donald, 33, 43, 59, 60, 64, 66, 68, 118, 121, 203
    January 6 insurrection, 184-185
    74 million votes, 184
    Attacks GOP candidates, 185
2014 vs. 2022 midterms, 198-203
2016 versus 2020 presidential vote, 89
2018 midterms, 42, 43-44, 45, 62-63, 65, 128, 132
U.S. Constitution, 12, 19
    Articles of Confederation, 20, 23
U.S. low global ranking in voting, 99-100
U.S. Supreme Court, 3, 19, 133, 148-149, 157, 175, 203
    Rules against congressional term limits, 20
    Upholds gay marriage, 74
    Roe Decision, 177-178
    Upholds ACA, 133
Voter suppression, 76-78, 92-96
    Restrictions, 148-149
    Language requirement, 95-96
    Congressional voter protection, 137-138
    Arizona legislature voter suppression, 151
Voting Rights Act, 137-138
    VRA history and challenges, 148-155
    Pre-clearance scrapped, 146, 156
Washington, George, 24, 26
Whites Voting against their interests, 11-12, 92, 112-113, 144-146

Wilson, Woodrow, 2
Women voters, 26, 122, 180, 198
Youth vote, 26, 97
    Youth disillusioned, 98-99

About the Author

Earl Ofari Hutchinson is the author of multiple books on race and politics in America. He is a political analyst. He has appeared on *MSNBC* and on *CNN*. His books include the trilogy on the Obama Years: *The Obama Legacy, How Obama Governed, The Year of Crisis and Challenge,* and *How Obama Won*. His most recent books are the *Trump Challenge to Black America* and *From King to Obama: Witness to a Turbulent History.* He is the publisher of thehutchinsonreport.net, a political issues web blog.